The List

By the Same Author

Evil and the Mountain: Ungreed
Project 2025: The Blueprint

Project 2025: The List

By
Esme Mees

An
Eatms Production

Copyright © 2024 Eatms Productions

All rights reserved.

No part of this book may be reproduced, or stored in a retrieval system, or transmitted in any form or by any means, electronic, mechanical, photocopying, recording, or otherwise, without express permission in writing from the publisher.

ISBN: 979-8-9909279-4-0

Cover, interior design, interior prints by: Esme Mees

eatms@pm.me
Printed in the United States of America.

Distrust everyone in whom the impulse to punish is powerful.

-Friedrich Nietzsche

Introduction

In the looming shadows of an uncertain future, *Project 2025: The List* is a succinct window into the insidious forces threatening to unravel the very fabric of our society. Each section, introduced with the stark, unforgiving lines of woodblock print illustrations, chronicles the myriad ways this ominous Christo-fascist Project 2025: Presidential Transition Project blueprint chips away at the pillars of democracy, social justice, and environmental sustainability. With every list detailing the silent and overt assaults on our world, *The List* is both a warning and a call to metaphorical arms for those willing to face the grim realities of our time- Project 2025 *is* the Republican agenda.

At the heart of this terrifying vision lies the Heritage Foundation's Mandate for Leadership under Project 2025. This initiative, cloaked in rhetoric of progress and patriotism, seeks to consolidate power in the hands of a few, steering policies that prioritize corporate interests and authoritarian governance. Its blueprint for leadership involves a radical overhaul of regulatory frameworks, dismantling protections that safeguard the environment, financial markets, and civil liberties. The goal is clear: to reshape America into a fortress of unfettered capitalism where the rich and powerful reign supreme, leaving the vulnerable to fend for themselves in an increasingly hostile landscape.

As we delve into the pages, the extent of the damage becomes painfully clear. We see the erosion of financial stability, the stark inequalities exacerbated by unbridled greed, and the devastating impacts on our climate, each list a stark reminder of the price we pay for the unchecked ambitions of the powerful. The once trusted institutions that upheld our democracy now appear as hollow shells, manipulated to serve the interests of a select few, leaving the majority vulnerable and disenfranchised. Internationally, the repercussions are equally dire. Alliances fray and global relations sour under the strain of policies that prioritize profit over people, and power over peace. *Project 2025: The List* serves as a mirror reflecting the dystopian trajectory we are hurtling towards. It implores us to confront these harsh truths and to rally against the forces that threaten to strip away our freedoms, our rights, and our hope for a just and equitable future.

Esme Mees, Summer 2024

Table of Contents

The Blueprint	10
Note on Section F	12
Note on the Incurious	15
Agriculture	17
Children	21
Climate	25
Crime	28
Education	33
Elections	37
Energy	41
Entertainment	45
Family	48
Finance	53
Government	57
Health	61
Housing.	64
Immigration	68
International	73
Justice	77
Labor	81
LGBTQ+	85
Media	88
Men	93
Military	97
Minorities	101
Religion	105

Taxes	109
Technology	113
Transportation	117
Veterans	121
Women	125
Note on Original Sin	129
Note on the Two Santa Clause Theory	133
Note on the GI Bill	137
Timeline of Money in Politics	141
Timeline of the Heritage Foundation	147
Timeline of the New Apostolic Reformation	153
Timeline of "Christian" Wars	157
Project 2025 Contributors	162
Individual Millionaire and Billionaire Backers	164
Note on Greed	167
In Conclusion	175
List of Prints	179
About the Author	181

The Blueprint

Project 2025 is a collection of far right "Christian" nationalist policy proposals designed to overhaul the U.S. government if a Republican wins the presidency in 2024. Created by the Heritage Foundation, this monstrous plan, 920 pages, aims to push a radical "Christian" nationalist agenda, stripping rights and protections. It is a nightmare scenario for democracy, civil liberties, international relations, and the environment.

Here is their plan-

Mandate for Leadership
The Conservative Promise
Project 2025: Presidential Transition Project

Acknowledgments
The Project Advisory Board
The 2025 Presidential Transition Project:
  A Note On "Project 2025"
Authors
Contributors
Forward: A Promise to America by Kevin Roberts

Section 1: Taking the Reins of Government
1. White House Office by Rick Dearborn
2. Executive Office of the President of the United States by Russ Vought
3. Central Personnel Agencies: Managing the Bureaucracy
   by Donald Devine, Dennis Dean Kirk, and Paul Dans

Section 2: The Common Defense Fund
4. Department of Defense by Christopher Miller
5. Department of Homeland Security by Ken Cuccinelli
6. Department of State by Kiron K. Skinner
7. Intelligence Community by Dustin J. Carmack
8. Media Agencies
   U.S. Agency for Global Media by Mora Namdar
   Corporation for Public Broadcasting by Mike Gonzalez
9. Agency for International Development by Max Primorac

Section 3: The General Welfare
10. Department of Agriculture by Daren Bakst
11. Department of Education by Lindsey M. Burke
12. Department of Energy & Related Commissions by Bernard L. McNamee
13. Environmental Protection Agency by Mandy M. Gunasekara
14. Department of Health and Human Services by Roger Severino
15. Department of Housing and Urban Development by Ben Carson
16. Department of the Interior by William Perry Pendley
17 Department of Justice by Gene Hamilton
18. Department of Labor & Related Agencies by Jonathon Berry
19. Department of Transportation by Diana Furchtgott-Roth
20. Department of Veterans Affairs by Brooks D. Tucker

Section 4: The Economy
21. Department of Commerce by Thomas F. Gilman
22. Department of the Treasury by William Walton, Stephan Moore, and David R. Burton
23. Export-Import Bank
    The Export-Import Bank Should Be Abolished by Veronique de Rugy
    The Case for the Export-Import Bank by Jennifer Hazelton
24. Federal Reserve by Paul Winfree
25. Small Business Administration by Karen Kerrigan
26. Trade
    The Case for Fair Trade by Peter Navarro
    The Case for Free Trade by Kent Lassman

Section 5: Independent Regulatory Agencies
27. Financial Regulatory Agencies
    Securities and Exchange Commission &
    Related Agencies by David R. Burton
    Consumer Protection Bureau by Robert Bowes
28. Federal Communications Commission By Brendan Carr
29. Federal Election Commission by Hans A. von Spakovsky
30. Federal Trade Commission by Adam Candeub

ONWARD! By Edwin Feulner

*Copyright The Heritage Foundation Project 2025

Note on Section F

Section F, a policy initiative begun under the Trump administration, marks a significant and troubling shift in the operation and ethos of the federal government. Ostensibly designed to streamline government operations and reduce inefficiencies, the policy allows for the reclassification of tens of thousands of federal employees into a new category, effectively making them at-will employees. This reclassification removes long-standing job protections and enables the administration to dismiss employees more easily, particularly those who are seen as disloyal or resistant to the president's agenda.

The underlying intent of Section F goes beyond simple bureaucratic reform. It is a strategic move to install loyalists throughout the federal workforce, ensuring that key positions are filled by individuals who are aligned with the administration's political objectives. This politicization of the civil service undermines the independence and impartiality that are crucial to a functioning democracy, turning what should be a non-partisan body into one that is increasingly driven by political loyalty. In addition to the direct impact on government employees, Section F fits into a broader strategy of reducing the visibility of government in areas that directly serve the public, such as regulatory agencies and social services, while maintaining or even expanding government functions that benefit wealthy corporations and elites. This approach is emblematic of a "socialism for the rich" mentality, where government resources and policies are skewed to favor the wealthiest at the expense of broader societal needs.

The policy's rhetoric of creating a smaller, more efficient government is misleading. While it might reduce the number of public-facing employees and services, it consolidates power within the executive branch, allowing for greater control and less oversight. This centralization of power raises concerns about potential abuses, cronyism, and the erosion of democratic checks and balances. Section F represents a dangerous precedent. It prioritizes political loyalty over public service, undermines the principles of meritocracy and impartiality in the federal workforce, and furthers the interests of a powerful elite at the expense of democratic governance and accountability. This policy not only threatens the livelihoods of federal employees but also jeopardizes the integrity and effectiveness of government institutions.

Note on the Incurious

The incurious nature of Christo-fascist patriarchal nostalgia is a driving force behind the regressive and anti-future thinking that defines many contemporary policies, particularly those championed by groups like The Heritage Foundation. This mentality is rooted in a fear of losing control and dominance in a world that is increasingly diverse and complex, and it clings to a past where white, male, and nominally Christian identities were unchallenged and held unquestioned authority.

At its core, this nostalgia is less about genuine heritage and more about a desire to return to a time when social hierarchies were rigid and beneficial to those at the top. The fear of a changing world—one where non-white, non-"Christian," and non-male voices are increasingly prominent—fuels this dogma. It promotes a worldview where any deviation from a narrow interpretation of tradition is seen as a threat, leading to policies that are not just resistant to change, but actively hostile to it. This anti-future mentality manifests in policies that undermine progress, whether it be in the realms of social justice, environmental sustainability, or technological innovation. These policies are designed to protect the status quo, ensuring that power remains concentrated in the hands of those who fit the Christo-fascist ideal of leadership: white, male, and outwardly "Christian." The result is a political and cultural movement that is deeply suspicious of diversity, equity, and the complexities of the modern world.

The irony of this mindset is that it claims to be rooted in protecting heritage, yet it is profoundly incurious about the true richness and diversity of American heritage itself. Instead of engaging with history in a way that acknowledges and learns from its full scope, this mentality selectively glorifies the past to justify its fear-driven policies. It seeks to freeze time, ignoring the inevitable march of progress and the growing interconnectedness of global societies. In essence, this Christo-fascist nostalgia is not about preserving heritage in any meaningful sense; it is about resisting a future where power is more evenly distributed and where the old hierarchies no longer dictate the terms of social, political, and economic life. Motivated by fear and an aversion to change, it crafts policies that are backward-looking, exclusionary, and ultimately detrimental to the future of a diverse and evolving society.

Agriculture

These categories and examples highlight the extensive and detrimental impact that Project 2025 and Republican's policies will have on agriculture, rural communities, and the broader food system in America. By rolling back essential protections, cutting critical funding, and ignoring the evolving needs of these sectors, Project 2025 and the Republicans threaten to undermine the sustainability, resilience, and prosperity of American agriculture and rural life.

Environmental Impact
1. Reducing Clean Water Act Protections: Allowing agricultural runoff and pollutants to contaminate water supplies.
2. Weakening Pesticide Regulations: Increasing the use of harmful chemicals that damage soil health and biodiversity.
3. Rolling Back Air Quality Standards: Permitting higher emissions from agricultural operations, negatively affecting both human and environmental health.
4. Cutting Funding for Soil Conservation Programs: Leading to soil erosion and reduced fertility, which diminishes crop yields.
5. Allowing Deforestation for Agricultural Expansion: Destroying forests that are essential for carbon sequestration.
6. Neglecting Climate Change Mitigation: Ignoring the impacts of climate change on farming, such as increased droughts.
7. Weakening Wetlands Protections: Draining wetlands, reducing natural flood control and harming wildlife habitats.
8. Encouraging Overuse of Water Resources: Promoting unsustainable irrigation practices, leading to water conflicts.
9. Reducing Protections Against Livestock Emissions: Increasing greenhouse gas emissions from animal agriculture.
10. Eliminating Support for Sustainable Farming Practices: Discouraging practices that maintain long-term soil health.

Economic Viability of Farms
1. Cutting Farm Subsidies for Small Farms: Favoring large agribusinesses, making it harder for family farms to compete.
2. Eliminating Crop Insurance Programs: Removing safety nets that protect farmers from market volatility and natural disasters.
3. Reducing Funding for Agricultural Research: Limiting innovation that could improve crop resilience and sustainability.
4. Encouraging Monoculture: Promoting single-crop farming, which

increases vulnerability to pests, diseases, and market shifts.
5. Allowing Foreign Entities to Purchase Farmland: Reducing domestic control over food production and driving up land prices.
6. Weakening Price Support Programs: Leaving farmers exposed to extreme price fluctuations, threatening their financial stability.
7. Reducing Access to Credit for Small Farmers: Making it difficult for small operations to secure loans necessary for growth.
8. Promoting Corporate Control of Agriculture: Consolidating market power with large companies, squeezing out smaller farms.
9. Cutting Disaster Relief for Farmers: Leaving farmers without financial support after catastrophic events.
10. Reducing Support for Organic Certification: Making it more difficult and costly for farmers to certify organic products.

Impact on Rural Communities
1. Cracking Down on Immigration: Reducing the availability of labor for farms, which rely on migrant workers for planting and harvesting.
2. Weakening Labor Protections: Decreasing safety standards and wages for farm workers, leading to exploitation and poor working conditions.
3. Reducing Healthcare Access in Rural Areas: Cutting funding for rural health clinics, leaving farm workers and their families.
4. Eliminating Education Programs for Farmworker Children: Limiting education and perpetuating cycles of poverty.
5. Allowing Child Labor in Agriculture: Relaxing restrictions, increasing the risk of children working in hazardous conditions.
6. Defunding Community Development Programs: Reducing investment in rural infrastructure, harming local economies.
7. Eliminating Housing Assistance for Migrant Workers: Increasing housing instability for essential agricultural labor.
8. Cutting Funding for Rural Broadband Expansion: Limiting access to digital tools and resources necessary for modern farming.
9. Weakening Support for Rural Schools: Reducing funding for education in rural areas, limiting future opportunities for children.
10. Disregard for Child Labor Protections: Increasing the risk of child labor in agriculture settings.

Food Security and Supply Chain Stability
1. Weakening Food Safety Regulations: Increasing the risk of foodborne illnesses and contamination in the supply chain.
2. Cutting Funding for Local Food Systems: Undermining farmers

markets, reducing access to fresh, local food.
3. Limiting Access to Export Markets: Implementing policies that hinder the ability of U.S. farmers to sell their products abroad.
4. Allowing Corporate Monopolies in the Food Industry: Concentrating control over food production and distribution.
5. Reducing Support for Emergency Food Aid Programs: Limiting resources for food assistance during crises.
6. Disrupting Trade Agreements: Creating instability in global food supply chains, affecting both imports and exports.
7. Cutting Investment in Agricultural Infrastructure: Leading to deterioration of roads, storage facilities, and transportation networks critical for food distribution.
8. Weakening Animal Welfare Standards: Allowing inhumane practices that can lead to lower quality meat and decreased trust.
9. Reducing Funding for Climate Adaptation in Agriculture: Leaving farmers unprepared for changing weather patterns.
10. Cutting Support for Food Innovation: Stifling advancements in farming methods and new food products and enhance food security.

Sustainability and Innovation in Agriculture
1. Relaxation of Food Safety Standards: Increasing the risk of foodborne illnesses in the food supply.
2. Eliminating Conservation Programs: Reducing incentives for practices that protect soil, water, and biodiversity.
3. Deregulation of GMOs: Reducing transparency and safety in food.
4. Elimination of Organic Certification Support: Undermining trust and integrity in organic farming.
5. Cutting Support for Organic Farming Research: Limiting advancements in organic sustainable farming techniques.
6. Reducing Incentives for Crop Diversification: Discouraging farmers from growing a variety of crops.
7. Weakening Water Conservation Efforts: Allowing inefficient water use practices that deplete water resources, critical in drought areas.
8. Neglect of Allergen Labeling: Putting consumers with food allergies at greater risk.
9. Reducing Support for Carbon Farming Initiatives: Limiting efforts to sequester carbon in agricultural soils.
10. Cuts to Food Inspection Services: Reducing oversight of food production processes, decreasing quality, increasing worker risks.

Children

These categories highlight the extensive and detrimental impact that Project 2025 and Republican's policies will have on the well-being and future of children in America. From education and healthcare to safety and economic stability, these policies threaten to undermine the basic foundations necessary for children to thrive.

Education
1. Defunding Public Schools: Diverting funds to private and charter schools, leaving public schools under-resourced and overcrowded.
2. Cutting Special Education Programs: Reducing support for children with disabilities, leading to inadequate education.
3. Elimination of Free School Meals: Ending programs that provide free or reduced-cost meals, increasing child hunger.
4. Reducing Funding for Early Childhood Education: Limiting access to preschool programs that are crucial for early development.
5. Censorship of Educational Content: Restricting the teaching of critical thinking and comprehensive history, including topics like racism and gender equality.
6. Limiting Access to Extracurricular Activities: Cutting funding for arts, sports, and after-school programs for holistic child development.
7. Increased Standardized Testing: Emphasizing test scores over creative and critical learning, stressful educational environment.
8. Cutting Mental Health Services in Schools: Reducing access to counseling for children struggling with mental health issues.
9. Eliminating Support for English Language Learners: Reducing programs that help non-English speaking children succeed in school.
10. Reducing Teacher Pay and Support: Leading to teacher shortages and lower educational quality for children.

Healthcare
1. Cuts to Medicaid and CHIP: Reducing access to essential healthcare services for low-income children.
2. Defunding Vaccination Programs: Increasing the risk of preventable diseases among children.
3. Eliminating Pediatric Health Research Funding: Slowing the development of treatments for childhood illnesses.
4. Reducing Mental Health Funding: Limiting access to services for children with mental health needs.
5. Restricting Access to Reproductive Health Services for Teens:

Leading to higher rates of teen pregnancy and STDs.
6. Cuts to Nutrition Assistance Programs: Reducing access to healthy food options for children in need.
7. Weakened Environmental Health Protections: Increasing exposure to pollutants that can harm children's development.
8. Eliminating School-Based Health Services: Reducing access to essential health care for children at school.
9. Neglect of Rural Health Initiatives: Exacerbating health disparities for children in rural areas.
10. Cuts to Disability Support Services: Reducing assistance for children with physical or developmental disabilities.

Child Welfare
1. Reducing Child Protective Services Funding: Decreasing resources to investigate and prevent child abuse and neglect.
2. Eliminating Family Support Programs: Cutting programs that provide parenting education and support to at-risk families.
3. Restricting Foster Care Services: Limiting resources for children in the foster care system, leading to poor outcomes.
4. Cutting Funding for Homeless Youth Programs: Reducing support for children who are homeless or in unstable housing.
5. Defunding After-School Programs: Leaving children without safe, structured environments after school.
6. Elimination of Child Care Subsidies: Making quality child care unaffordable for many families.
7. Criminalizing Juvenile Behavior: Increasing the incarceration of children for minor offenses, rather than providing support and rehabilitation.
8. Cuts to Domestic Violence Programs: Reducing protections for children living in abusive households.
9. Weakened Labor Protections: Increasing the risk of child labor in some communities.
10. Reducing Immigration Services for Children: Denying support and protections for immigrant children, including those separated from their families.

Social and Economic Policies
1. Cuts to Social Security for Children: Reducing benefits for children who rely on Social Security due to the death or disability of a parent.
2. Elimination of the Child Tax Credit: Increasing financial strain on families, leading to higher rates of child poverty.

3. Reducing Funding for Housing Assistance: Increasing child homelessness and housing instability.
4. Cuts to Food Assistance Programs: Reducing SNAP benefits, leading to higher rates of child hunger and malnutrition.
5. Increasing Barriers to Welfare Assistance: Making it harder for families to access temporary assistance, pushing children into poverty.
6. Raising Barriers to Disability Benefits: Making it more difficult for families with disabled children to access financial support.
7. Eliminating Affordable Housing Initiatives: Limiting the availability of safe and affordable housing for families with children.
8. Cuts to Energy Assistance Programs: Leaving families unable to afford heating or cooling, putting children's health at risk.
9. Reducing Minimum Wage Protections: Lowering family income, increasing economic instability for children.
10. Neglect of Urban Programs: Ignoring the needs of children in impoverished urban areas, leading to unsafe living conditions.

Safety and Legal Protections
1. Weakened Gun Control Laws: Increasing the risk of gun violence in schools and communities.
2. Cuts to Juvenile Justice Reform Programs: Reducing resources for programs that keep children out of the criminal justice system.
3. Weakening of Child Labor Laws: Allowing younger children to work in dangerous and exploitative conditions.
4. Reduction in Anti-Trafficking Programs: Increasing the vulnerability of children to human trafficking and exploitation.
5. Eliminating Internet Safety Programs: Leaving children more exposed to online predators and cyberbullying.
6. Reducing Traffic Safety Initiatives: Increasing the risk of accidents and fatalities among child pedestrians and cyclists.
7. Cuts to Emergency Preparedness Programs: Leaving schools and communities less prepared for natural disasters and emergencies.
8. Weakening of Consumer Product Safety Regulations: Allowing dangerous toys and products to reach the market.
9. Neglect of Anti-Bullying Programs: Increasing the incidence of bullying and its harmful effects on children's mental health.
10. Reduction in Public Safety Funding: Compromising the safety of communities where children live and play.

Climate

These categories and examples illustrate how Project 2025 and Republican's policies will harm the climate, exacerbate environmental degradation, and endanger public health and ecosystem stability, ultimately leading to long-term damage to the planet and its inhabitants, as lying about climate change as a hoax harms the planet.

Environmental Deregulation
1. Rollback of Clean Air Act Protections: Increased emissions of greenhouse gases, worsening air quality, and climate change.
2. Weakening of Clean Water Act Standards: Permitting more pollutants to enter waterways, ecosystems and water resources.
3. Deregulation of Industrial Emissions: Removing restrictions on emissions from factories and power plants.
4. Relaxation of Vehicle Emissions Standards: Higher emissions from cars and trucks, increasing pollution and carbon output.
5. Loosening Restrictions on Methane Emissions: Enabling more methane, a potent greenhouse gas, to be released from oil operations.
6. Deregulation of Chemical Manufacturing: Increasing the release of harmful chemicals that degrade the ozone layer.
7. Weakening of Hazardous Waste Disposal Regulations: Increasing the risk of environmental contamination and pollution.
8. Reduction in Enforcement of Environmental Laws: Decreasing oversight and accountability for environmental violations.
9. Elimination of the National Environmental Policy Act (NEPA) Requirements: Removing the need for federal agencies to consider environmental impacts before proceeding with projects.
10. Deregulation of Pesticide Use: Allowing greater use of harmful pesticides, damaging ecosystems and contributing to biodiversity loss.

Fossil Fuel Expansion
1. Opening Public Lands to Oil and Gas Drilling: Increasing fossil fuel extraction and its associated environmental damage.
2. Reversing Protections for Arctic Drilling: Allowing drilling in fragile Arctic ecosystems, threatening wildlife and climate change.
3. Encouraging Coal Production: Promoting coal mining and usage, the dirtiest form of energy in terms of carbon emissions.
4. Elimination of Subsidies for Renewable Energy: Shifting financial support away from clean energy sources toward fossil fuels.
5. Expansion of Offshore Drilling: Increasing the risk of oil spills and

environmental damage to marine ecosystems.
6. Approval of New Pipeline Projects: Facilitating the transportation of oil and gas across the country, increasing fossil fuel dependence.
7. Reducing Royalty Rates for Fossil Fuel Extraction on Public Lands: Making it cheaper for companies to exploit public resources, leading to more extraction.
8. Expanding Fracking Operations: Increasing the use of hydraulic fracturing, which contaminates water supplies and emits methane.
9. Weakening Regulations on Mountaintop Removal Mining: Allowing mining practices that devastate landscapes and ecosystems.
10. Supporting the Export of Fossil Fuels: Increasing global dependence on fossil fuels, exacerbating climate change globally.

Climate Policy Rollbacks
1. Withdrawal from the Paris Agreement: Abandoning international commitments to reduce greenhouse gas emissions.
2. Eliminating Federal Climate Change Research Programs: Reducing climate change impacts and how to mitigate them.
3. Defunding Climate Adaptation Initiatives: Leaving communities vulnerable to the impacts of climate change, such as rising sea levels and extreme weather.
4. Cuts to the Environmental Protection Agency (EPA): Reducing the agency's ability to regulate and enforce environmental protections.
5. Blocking State-Level Climate Initiatives: Preventing states from implementing their own climate policies and regulations.
6. Elimination of Carbon Pricing Mechanisms: Removing economic incentives for reducing carbon emissions.
7. Defunding Renewable Energy Research and Development: Slowing the advancement of clean energy technologies.
8. Ending Tax Credits for Electric Vehicles: Discouraging the adoption of cleaner transportation options.
9. Cuts to Public Transit Funding: Encouraging car dependency, increasing emissions from transportation.
10. Elimination of Federal Support for Green Building Standards: Discouraging energy-efficient construction practices.

Biodiversity and Ecosystem Destruction
1. Reduction in Protected Land Designations: Opening up national monuments and protected areas to development and extraction.
2. Weakening Endangered Species Act Protections: Allowing more habitat destruction and threatening biodiversity.

3. Deregulation of Logging in National Forests: Increasing deforestation and habitat loss, reducing carbon sequestration.
4. Encouraging Agricultural Expansion into Forested Areas: Leading to deforestation and loss of carbon sinks.
5. Allowing Destruction of Wetlands: Removing protections for wetlands that act as crucial carbon sinks and biodiversity hotspots.
6. Supporting Large-Scale Industrial Agriculture: Farming practices that lead to soil degradation, deforestation, and biodiversity loss.
7. Reduction in Marine Protected Areas: Opening oceans to overfishing and mining, harming marine ecosystems.
8. Deregulation of Mining Practices: Increasing habitat destruction and pollution in sensitive ecosystems.
9. Encouraging Overgrazing on Public Lands: Leading to desertification and loss of grasslands that store carbon.
10. Ignoring Invasive Species Threats: Allowing invasive species to spread, disrupting ecosystems and reducing biodiversity.

Public Health and Climate Resilience
1. Elimination of Climate Change Health Initiatives: Ignoring the public health impacts of climate change, such as heatwaves and increased disease transmission.
2. Cuts to Disaster Preparedness Programs: Leaving communities less prepared for climate-induced disasters like hurricanes and wildfires.
3. Reducing Funding for Climate Resilient Infrastructure: Failing to invest in infrastructure that can withstand extreme weather events.
4. Neglecting Urban Heat Island Mitigation Programs: Exacerbating health risks in cities due to increased temperatures.
5. Ending Support for Flood Prevention Programs: Increasing the risk of flooding in vulnerable areas.
6. Defunding Community Resilience Initiatives: Reducing support for local projects that help communities adapt to climate impacts.
7. Cutting Funding for Public Health Emergency Response: Weakening the response to climate-related health emergencies.
8. Ignoring Climate Change in Zoning and Urban Planning: Leading to unsustainable development that is vulnerable to climate impacts.
9. Deregulation of Coastal Development: Increasing vulnerability to sea-level rise and storm surges.
10. Reducing Support for Water Conservation Programs: Exacerbating drought conditions in climate-affected regions.

Crime

These categories and examples illustrate the extensive ways in which Project 2025 and Republican's policies will compromise safety, exacerbate crime, and weaken the mechanisms in place to protect individuals and society from criminal activity, both domestically and globally.

Domestic Safety and Crime
1. Weakening Gun Control Laws: Increasing the availability of firearms, leading to higher rates of gun violence and mass shootings.
2. Reducing Funding for Community Policing: Limiting proactive, community-based approaches that prevent crime.
3. Cuts to Domestic Violence Programs: Reducing support for survivors and prevention efforts, leading to increased incidents of domestic violence.
4. Dismantling Mental Health Services: Leaving individuals with untreated mental health issues, which can lead to criminal behavior.
5. Eliminating Support for Anti-Gang Initiatives: Allowing gang activity to flourish unchecked in vulnerable communities.
6. Relaxing Drug Enforcement: Leading to an increase in drug-related crimes and addiction.
7. Defunding Juvenile Justice Programs: Increasing the likelihood of youth turning to crime without rehabilitation or support.
8. Reducing Access to Legal Aid: Limiting the ability of low-income individuals to defend themselves, leading to unjust outcomes and higher incarceration rates.
9. Neglecting School Safety Programs: Increasing the risk of violence and crime within educational institutions.
10. Weakening Protections for Crime Victims: Making it harder for victims to receive justice and support and underreporting of crimes.

International Crime and Terrorism
1. Reduction in Counterterrorism Funding: Weakening the ability to prevent and respond to terrorist threats globally.
2. Cuts to Foreign Aid: Destabilizing regions and creating environments where crime and terrorism can thrive.
3. Neglect of Cybersecurity Measures: Leaving the country vulnerable to cyberattacks from international criminals and state actors.
4. Relaxing Sanctions on Rogue States: Allowing them to finance terrorism and criminal enterprises more easily.

5. Withdrawal from International Crime-Fighting Organizations: Reducing collaboration with global partners in combating crime.
6. Cutting Diplomatic Security Programs: Increasing risks to diplomats and international representatives.
7. Weakened Intelligence Sharing Agreements: Limiting the exchange of critical information that prevents crimes and terrorism.
8. Reduction in Border Security Measures: Increasing the risk of smuggling, trafficking, and cross-border crime.
9. Scaling Back Peacekeeping Efforts: Allowing conflicts to fester and escalate into larger, more dangerous criminal enterprises.
10. Elimination of Support for Anti-Trafficking Programs: Increasing the prevalence of human trafficking and related crimes globally.

White-Collar Crime
1. Deregulating Financial Industries: Encouraging unethical behavior and increasing the risk of financial fraud and Ponzi schemes.
2. Weakening Anti-Money Laundering Regulations: Making it easier for criminals to launder money through legitimate financial systems.
3. Reducing Oversight of Corporate Governance: Allowing executives to engage in fraudulent activities with less fear of repercussions.
4. Relaxing Environmental Regulations: Enabling corporations to engage in illegal pollution and environmental crimes legally.
5. Cutting Funding for Regulatory Agencies: Reducing the ability to investigate and prosecute white-collar crimes.
6. Loosening Campaign Finance Laws: Increasing the potential for corruption and the influence of dirty money in politics.
7. Weakened Consumer Protection Laws: Allowing businesses to engage in predatory practices without facing legal consequences.
8. Eliminating Whistleblower Protections: Discouraging individuals from reporting corporate wrongdoing.
9. Defunding Securities and Exchange Commission (SEC): Limiting the oversight of financial markets and increasing the potential for stock market manipulation.
10. Reducing Penalties for Corporate Crime: Making it less costly for companies to engage in illegal activities, increasing malfeasance.

Cybercrime and Data Security
1. Neglecting Cybersecurity Infrastructure: Leaving critical infrastructure vulnerable to cyberattacks, which can disrupt services.
2. Reducing Funding for Cybercrime Enforcement: Limiting the ability to track and prosecute online criminal activities.

3. Weakening Data Privacy Protections: Making personal and corporate data more susceptible to theft and exploitation.
4. Eliminating Support for Cybersecurity Education and Training: Leading to a shortage of skilled professionals to defend against threats.
5. Lack of Investment in Secure Technology: Increasing the risk of data breaches and hacking incidents.
6. Deregulation of Tech Industries: Allowing tech companies to evade responsibility for data protection and security breaches.
7. Cutting Collaboration with International Cybersecurity Agencies: Reducing the effectiveness of global efforts to combat cybercrime.
8. Encouraging Data Collection Without Safeguards: Increasing the risk of sensitive data being misused or stolen.
9. Weakened Intellectual Property Protections: Facilitating the theft of proprietary technology and trade secrets.
10. Ignoring the Threat of State-Sponsored Cybercrime: Allowing foreign governments to conduct cyber espionage with impunity.

Corporate and Environmental Crime
1. Deregulating Environmental Protections: Allowing corporations to engage in illegal dumping, pollution, and other environmental crimes.
2. Relaxing Workplace Safety Standards: Leading to increased accidents and fatalities, which are often covered up by employers.
3. Eliminating Accountability for Corporate Polluters: Reducing legal consequences for companies that harm the environment.
4. Weakened Enforcement of Labor Laws: Enabling businesses to exploit workers through wage theft, unsafe working conditions, and other illegal practices.
5. Cutting Funding for Environmental Crime Units: Limiting the ability to investigate and prosecute environmental violations.
6. Encouraging Resource Exploitation in Protected Areas: Increasing illegal logging, mining, and wildlife trafficking.
7. Ignoring Corporate Tax Evasion: Allowing companies to evade taxes, leading to reduced public revenue and increasing the burden on honest taxpayers.
8. Loosening Restrictions on Corporate Mergers: Enabling monopolistic practices that harm consumers and stifle competition.
9. Reducing Penalties for Regulatory Noncompliance: Making it easier for companies to violate laws without significant consequences.
10. Weakened Enforcement of Anti-Bribery Laws: Increasing the incidence of corruption and bribery in business dealings, both domestically and internationally.

Education

These categories and examples illustrate the extensive ways in which Project 2025 and Republican's policies will harm all levels of education, from early childhood through higher education, by reducing access, resources, and support for students, teachers, and educational institutions. These harmful policies not only threaten the quality of education but also deepen inequities, leaving vulnerable students and communities at an even greater disadvantage, and undermining the future potential of an entire generation.

Early Childhood Education
1. Cuts to Head Start Programs: Reducing access to early childhood education for low-income families.
2. Defunding Pre-K Initiatives: Limiting early learning opportunities that are crucial for child development.
3. Elimination of Subsidies for Childcare Centers: Making early education unaffordable for many families.
4. Reducing Funding for Early Intervention Services: Harming children with developmental delays by limiting access to necessary support.
5. Deregulation of Childcare Standards: Allowing lower quality care in early childhood education settings.
6. Eliminating Nutrition Programs for Preschoolers: Reducing access to healthy meals, impacting learning and development.
7. Limiting Access to Special Education Services: Reducing early support for children with disabilities.
8. Cuts to Family Engagement Programs: Undermining parental involvement in early education.
9. Reducing Support for Early Literacy Programs: Decreasing access to foundational reading and language skills.
10. Elimination of Professional Development for Early Childhood Educators: Lowering the quality of teaching in early childhood settings.

K-12 Education
1. Defunding Public Schools: Diverting funds to private and charter schools, leaving public schools under-resourced.
2. Eliminating Support for Arts and Music Programs: Cutting essential creative outlets that enhance student learning.
3. Increasing Standardized Testing Requirements: Shifting focus from

holistic education to test preparation.
4. Cutting Funding for Special Education Services: Reducing resources for students with disabilities.
5. Reducing Teacher Salaries and Benefits: Leading to teacher shortages and lower quality education.
6. Censorship of Curriculum Content: Restricting teaching on important topics like history, science, and social justice.
7. Closing Schools in Low-Income Areas: Forcing students to travel further or attend overcrowded schools.
8. Elimination of Free School Meal Programs: Increasing hunger and decreasing academic performance among students.
9. Limiting Access to School Counseling Services: Reducing support for students' mental health and academic guidance.
10. Cuts to After-School Programs: Removing opportunities for additional learning and safe environments for students.

Higher Education
1. Cuts to Pell Grants and Financial Aid: Making college less affordable for low-income students.
2. Defunding Public Universities: Increasing tuition costs and reducing access to higher education.
3. Eliminating Student Loan Forgiveness Programs: Saddling graduates with unmanageable debt.
4. Cuts to Research Funding: Limiting opportunities for academic research and innovation.
5. Privatization of University Services: Increasing costs and reducing access to essential services on campus.
6. Reducing Support for Community Colleges: Limiting affordable pathways to higher education for non-traditional students.
7. Elimination of Diversity and Inclusion Programs: Creating a less supportive environment for marginalized students.
8. Limiting Academic Freedom: Censoring curriculum and research topics in higher education institutions.
9. Cuts to Graduate Education Funding: Reducing support for students pursuing advanced degrees.
10. Increased Reliance on Adjunct Faculty: Leading to lower job security and quality of education in colleges and universities.

Teacher and Staff Support
1. Cuts to Teacher Professional Development Programs: Reducing opportunities for teachers to improve their skills and effectiveness.

2. Reducing Teacher Salaries and Benefits: Leading to burnout, higher turnover rates, and less experienced educators.
3. Eliminating Support for Teacher Unions: Weakening collective bargaining power for fair wages and working conditions.
4. Limiting Resources for Classroom Supplies: Forcing teachers to pay out of pocket for essential teaching materials.
5. Cuts to School Support Staff: Increasing the workload on teachers and reducing student support.
6. Elimination of Mental Health Resources for Educators: Ignoring the stress and challenges faced by teaching staff.
7. Reducing Hiring Budgets: Leading to larger class sizes and less individualized attention for students.
8. Cuts to Substitute Teacher Funding: Creating classroom disruptions when regular teachers are absent.
9. Defunding Teacher Preparation Programs: Lowering the quality of new educators entering the workforce.
10. Increased Workload Without Compensation: Leading to teacher burnout and a decline in the quality of education.

Educational Equity and Access
1. Elimination of Affirmative Action in Admissions: Reducing diversity in higher education institutions.
2. Cuts to Bilingual Education Programs: Limiting access to education for non-English speaking students.
3. Reducing Support for Students with Disabilities: Making education less accessible for students requiring special services.
4. Defunding Title I Programs: Ending funds for low-income students.
5. Eliminating School Transportation Programs: Making it harder for students in rural or low-income areas to attend school.
6. Cuts to Internet and Technology Access Programs: Increasing the digital divide and limiting access to online learning resources.
7. Defunding School Nutrition Programs: Exacerbating food insecurity and hindering student performance.
8. Reducing Funding for STEM Initiatives: Limiting opportunities for students to engage in science, technology, engineering, and math.
9. Eliminating College Preparatory Programs: Reducing support for first-generation and low-income students aiming for higher education.
10. Weakening Anti-Discrimination Policies: Allowing biases to flourish, making schools less safe and welcoming for all students.

Elections

These categories and examples demonstrate how Project 2025 and Republican's policies will undermine the integrity, accessibility, and fairness of elections, threatening the democratic process at multiple levels. Such actions collectively weaken the principles of democracy, disenfranchising voters, and eroding public trust in the system.

Voter Suppression
1. Implementation of Strict Voter ID Laws: Making it harder for marginalized groups to vote by requiring burdensome identification.
2. Reduction of Early Voting: Limiting the number of early voting days, reducing access for those with inflexible schedules.
3. Elimination of Same-Day Voter Registration: Removing the ability for voters to register on Election Day, disenfranchising late registrants.
4. Closing Polling Stations in Minority Areas: Forcing voters in these areas to travel long distances or face long wait times.
5. Purging Voter Rolls: Removing eligible voters from the rolls without adequate notice, particularly targeting minorities and low-income individuals.
6. Gerrymandering: Redrawing electoral districts to dilute the voting power of certain groups.
7. Reduction of Mail-In Voting: Limiting access to absentee ballots, which disproportionately affects elderly, disabled, and rural voters.
8. Restricting Ballot Drop Boxes: Reducing the number of ballot drop boxes, making it harder for voters to submit their ballots securely.
9. Limiting Language Assistance: Reducing support for non-English-speaking voters, making it harder for them to navigate the process.
10. Intimidation at Polling Places: Allowing aggressive monitoring or open carry at polling places, which can intimidate voters.

Election Integrity
1. Disbanding Independent Election Commissions: Undermining nonpartisan bodies that oversee fair election practices.
2. Politicization of Election Officials: Appointing partisan loyalists to key election oversight roles, risking biased administration.
3. Reducing Funding for Election Security: Leaving voting systems vulnerable to hacking and other security threats.
4. Relaxing Campaign Finance Laws: Increasing the influence of money in elections, allowing wealthy individuals and corporations to have outsized influence.

5. Blocking Election Audits: Preventing independent audits that ensure the accuracy of election results.
6. Spreading Misinformation About Election Processes: Undermining trust in the electoral system by spreading false information.
7. Reducing Transparency in Vote Counting: Limiting observers' access to the vote-counting process, raising doubts about fairness.
8. Weakening Penalties for Election Interference: Reducing consequences for attempts to manipulate the election process.
9. Allowing Foreign Influence: Failing to address or counteract foreign attempts to interfere in U.S. elections.
10. Refusing to Certify Election Results: Politically motivated refusals to certify legitimate election outcomes, undermining democracy.

Voter Access and Participation
1. Reducing Polling Hours: Limiting the time polls are open, making it harder for working people to vote.
2. Cutting Back on Voter Education Programs: Reducing efforts to inform voters about how, where, and when to vote.
3. Eliminating Automatic Voter Registration: Forcing voters to navigate more complex registration processes, decreasing registration.
4. Limiting Accessibility for Disabled Voters: Reducing accommodations and access for voters with disabilities.
5. Cutting Translation Services: Making it difficult for non-English speakers to access voting materials and information.
6. Restricting Voting Rights for Formerly Incarcerated Individuals: Implementing policies that permanently disenfranchise individuals with past felony convictions.
7. Discouraging Student Voting: Creating barriers for students who may wish to vote in their college town rather than their home state.
8. Eliminating Voting Rights for Certain Demographics: Proposing laws that disproportionately affect minorities, youth, and low-income.
9. Closing Voting Locations in Rural Areas: Increasing the difficulty of voting for people living in remote areas.
10. Discouraging Vote-by-Mail: Creating hurdles for voters who rely on mail-in ballots, such as requiring unnecessary forms of verification.

Electoral System Manipulation
1. Undermining the Electoral College: Proposing changes that could skew the electoral college to favor certain outcomes.
2. Pushing for Legislative Control Over Electors: Allowing state legislatures to override the popular vote by appointing fake electors.

3. Promoting Voter ID Laws with Narrow Criteria: Implementing ID laws that unfairly target minorities and lower-income voters.
4. Supporting Partisan Redistricting: Endorsing gerrymandering to maintain or increase political control in various regions.
5. Reducing Ballot Access for Third-Party Candidates: Implementing rules that make it harder for third-party candidates to get on the ballot, limiting voter choices.
6. Implementing Closed Primaries: Restricting voting to registered party members, excluding independent or non-affiliated voters.
7. Manipulating Voter Eligibility Criteria: Changing eligibility requirements to disenfranchise specific groups.
8. Promoting "Faithless Electors": Encouraging electors to vote against their state's popular vote.
9. Delaying or Canceling Elections: Justifying delays or cancellations of elections under dubious circumstances.
10. Encouraging Spoiler Candidates: Promoting candidates with no chance of winning to split the vote and manipulate outcomes.

Technology and Voting Security
1. Neglecting Voting Machine Upgrades: Leaving outdated, insecure voting machines in use, increasing the risk of errors or tampering.
2. Allowing the Use of Unverified Voting Software: Permitting the use of software that hasn't been thoroughly vetted for security.
3. Ignoring the Need for Paper Ballots: Failing to require paper backups for electronic voting, making recounts and audits difficult.
4. Reducing Cybersecurity Measures for Voting Systems: Cutting funding for cybersecurity protections, making hacking more likely.
5. Eliminating Funding for Election Cybersecurity Training: Leaving election officials unable to prevent and respond to cyber threats.
6. Weakening Voter Data Protection: Making voter registration data more susceptible to breaches and misuse.
7. Ignoring Threats from Deepfake Technology: Allowing misinformation campaigns to use technology to mislead voters.
8. Lack of Regulation for Online Political Advertising: Permitting deceptive or manipulative ads to influence voters without oversight.
9. Allowing Online Voting Without Adequate Safeguards: Proposing online voting options without addressing the security risks involved.
10. Failing to Address Social Media Manipulation: Ignoring the influence of social media bots and disinformation campaigns on public opinion and voter behavior.

Energy

The policies of Project 2025 and Republicans undermine the shift to clean energy by cutting support for renewables, rolling back efficiency measures, and increasing reliance on fossil fuels. These actions escalate greenhouse gas emissions, weaken climate change initiatives, and compromise energy security.

Renewable Energy Development
1. Cutting Funding for Renewable Energy Research: Reducing investment in solar, wind, and other renewable energy technologies.
2. Eliminating Tax Credits for Renewable Energy: Making renewable energy projects less financially viable.
3. Rolling Back Renewable Portfolio Standards: Removing state-level mandates that require a certain percentage of energy to come from renewable sources.
4. Reducing Incentives for Clean Energy Production: Decreasing support for businesses and homeowners to install renewable systems.
5. Defunding Public-Private Partnerships in Renewable Energy: Limiting collaboration between government and the private sector.
6. Opposing New Renewable Energy Projects: Blocking or delaying the approval of new solar and wind farms.
7. Weakening Federal Support for Offshore Wind Development: Slowing the growth of offshore wind energy.
8. Reducing Funding for Battery Storage Technology: Hampering the development of technologies necessary to store renewable energy for when it's needed most.
9. Curtailing Investment in Grid Modernization: Preventing upgrades that would allow the grid to better handle renewable energy inputs.
10. Undermining Support for Distributed Energy Resources: Discouraging the adoption of localized renewable energy systems.

Fossil Fuel Dependence
1. Expanding Fossil Fuel Extraction on Public Lands: Opening more federal lands to oil, gas, and coal extraction, increasing emissions.
2. Reducing Regulations on Fossil Fuel Industries: Allowing more pollution and environmental degradation from coal, oil, and gas.
3. Subsidizing Fossil Fuel Companies: Providing financial incentives that keep dirty energy sources economically viable.
4. Reversing Bans on New Fossil Fuel Infrastructure: Supporting the construction of new pipelines, refineries, and export facilities.

5. Encouraging Coal Production: Promoting one of the most carbon-intensive energy sources.
6. Weakening Methane Emission Regulations: Allowing natural gas producers to release more methane, a potent greenhouse gas.
7. Cutting Funding for Fossil Fuel Alternatives: Limiting research and development of cleaner, more sustainable energy options.
8. Promoting Fracking Expansion: Increasing the use of hydraulic fracturing, which has significant environmental and health risks.
9. Removing Restrictions on Offshore Drilling: Expanding oil drilling in sensitive ocean areas, threatening marine ecosystems.
10. Supporting International Fossil Fuel Projects: Financing fossil fuel extraction projects in other countries, exacerbating climate change.

Energy Efficiency
1. Rolling Back Fuel Efficiency Standards: Allowing cars and trucks to consume more fuel and emit more pollution.
2. Reducing Support for Energy-Efficient Appliances: Ending programs that encourage the adoption of energy-saving devices.
3. Defunding Weatherization Assistance Programs: Making it harder for low-income families to improve the energy efficiency of homes.
4. Weakening Building Energy Codes: Allowing new buildings to be constructed without modern energy efficiency standards.
5. Eliminating Energy Star Program: Cutting the program that certifies and promotes energy-efficient products.
6. Reducing Funding for Public Transit: Encouraging car dependency and increasing overall energy consumption.
7. Cutting Support for Energy-Efficient Industrial Practices: Making it less attractive for industries to invest in energy-saving technologies.
8. Opposing New Efficiency Standards for Commercial Buildings: Limiting progress in reducing energy use in large buildings.
9. Reducing Investment in Smart Grid Technology: Hampering efforts to create a more efficient, responsive electricity grid.
10. Ending Incentives for High-Efficiency Vehicles: Discouraging the adoption of electric and hybrid vehicles that reduce fuel consumption.

Climate Change and Environmental Impact
1. Weakening Emission Reduction Targets: Scaling back commitments to reduce greenhouse gas emissions, increasing risk.
2. Eliminating Climate Action Plans: Abandoning strategies that integrate renewable energy as part of a broader climate solution.
3. Reducing Funding for Climate Research: Limiting the ability to

understand and mitigate the impacts of energy production.
4. Encouraging Carbon-Intensive Industries: Supporting industries that are significant contributors to global warming.
5. Rolling Back Protections for Vulnerable Ecosystems: Allowing energy projects to destroy critical habitats and biodiversity loss.
6. Cutting International Climate Funding: Reducing financial support for global initiatives to combat climate change.
7. Opposing Carbon Pricing Mechanisms: Preventing the implementation of taxes or trading systems that would incentivize reductions in carbon emissions.
8. Promoting the Use of High-Carbon Fuels: Encouraging the use of tar sands, oil shale, and other carbon-intensive fuels.
9. Reducing Support for Urban Planning Initiatives: Discouraging development practices that integrate energy efficiency and resilience.
10. Dismantling Clean Power Plan: Removing a key policy that set national limits on carbon emissions from power plants.

Energy Independence and Security
1. Neglecting Investment in Domestic Clean Energy: Reducing renewable energy sources, making the U.S. rely on foreign fossil fuels.
2. Reducing Strategic Energy Reserves: Decreasing the stockpiles of essential energy resources, leaving the nation open to disruptions.
3. Undermining Energy Diplomacy: Reducing collaboration with other countries on energy security and climate goals.
4. Opposing Renewable Energy Exports: Limiting the U.S.'s ability to become a leader in global renewable energy markets.
5. Supporting Energy Monopolies: Allowing companies to control production and distribution, stifling innovation.
6. Reducing Investment in Energy Resilience: Failing to prepare the energy grid for extreme weather events.
7. Curtailing Support for Decentralized Energy Production: Making it harder for communities to generate their own renewable energy.
8. Weakening Cybersecurity for Energy Infrastructure: Leaving critical energy infrastructure vulnerable to cyberattacks.
9. Limiting Research on Next-Generation Energy Technologies: Stifling innovation in emerging energy fields like fusion and nuclear.
10. Reducing Public Involvement in Energy Policy: Limiting transparency and public input in energy decision-making, leading to policies that favor special interests.

Entertainment

Project 2025 and Republican's approach to entertainment imposes strict censorship, restricts creative freedom, and limits public access to diverse content. By legislating morality and consolidating media control, it stifles innovation and reduces the richness of cultural expression. These policies undermine freedom of expression resulting in a controlled and less interesting, dynamic, and vibrant society.

Censorship and Content Restrictions
1. Imposing Strict Censorship Laws: Limiting creative freedom by banning or restricting content deemed "immoral" or "offensive."
2. Mandating Content Ratings Based on Religious Standards: Enforcing ratings that reflect specific moral or religious viewpoints.
3. Banning LGBTQ+ Representation: Removing or restricting content that includes LGBTQ+ characters or themes.
4. Prohibiting Depictions of Non-Traditional Families: Limiting portrayals of diverse family structures in film, TV, and literature.
5. Censoring Content that Criticizes Government or Authority: Silencing dissenting voices and reducing the diversity of perspectives.
6. Restricting Artistic Expression in Music and Art: Limiting the ability of artists to explore controversial or challenging themes.
7. Censoring Political Satire: Suppressing comedic and satirical content that critiques political figures or policies.
8. Enforcing Blasphemy Laws: Banning content that challenges or critiques religious beliefs, stifling freedom of expression.
9. Restricting Access to Mature Content: Imposing broad restrictions on adult-oriented content, even for consenting adults.
10. Limiting International Content: Reducing access to foreign films, music, and literature that offer diverse cultural perspectives.

Control of Media and Broadcasting
1. Consolidating Media Ownership: Allowing corporations to control the majority of media outlets, reducing diversity of content.
2. Mandating Religious or Moral Programming: Requiring broadcasters to air content that aligns with moral or religious values.
3. Defunding Public Broadcasting: Reducing funding for public television and radio, access to educational and diverse content.
4. Restricting Streaming Services: Imposing regulations that limit the content available on streaming platforms.
5. Reducing Support for Independent Films: Cutting grants and

funding for independent filmmakers, leading to a dominance of mainstream, sanitized content.
6. Banning Certain Genres or Topics: Prohibiting the production or airing of content that explores taboo or controversial issues.
7. Censorship of Social Media Platforms: Forcing platforms to remove content that doesn't align with government-approved standards.
8. Requiring Political Neutrality in Media: Imposing strict regulations that prevent media from taking stances on social and political issues.
9. Encouraging Self-Censorship: Pressuring media companies to avoid producing content deemed controversial, to avoid penalties.
10. Limiting Foreign Media Influence: Restricting the import and broadcast of international media that may conflict cultural policies.

Impact on Creative Industries
1. Reducing Funding for Arts and Culture: Slashing government support for arts programs, festivals, and cultural institutions.
2. Imposing Morality Clauses in Contracts: Forcing artists and creators to adhere to strict moral guidelines or risk losing contracts.
3. Restricting Funding for Controversial Projects: Denying grants and subsidies to projects that deal with sensitive or controversial topics.
4. Promoting Traditional Values in Entertainment: Encouraging content that reinforces traditional gender roles and family structures.
5. Diminishing Artistic Freedom in Education: Limiting the scope of arts education to exclude experimental or controversial works.
6. Imposing Fines for Non-Compliant Content: Financially penalizing creators and producers who violate moral or content guidelines.
7. Censorship of Public Art: Removing or altering public art installations that are considered offensive or inappropriate.
8. Restricting Creative Licenses: Tightening regulations on who can produce, distribute, or perform artistic works.
9. Curtailing International Artistic Collaborations: Limiting partnerships with foreign artists and exchange of cultural works.
10. Restricting Access to Funding for Minority Artists: Reducing funding opportunities for artists from marginalized communities.

Audience Access and Participation
1. Banning Certain Films or Shows from Theaters and TV: Preventing the public from accessing content deemed inappropriate by government standards.
2. Restricting Content Access Based on Age: Imposing stricter age restrictions on accessing certain types of entertainment.

3. Imposing Internet Filters on Content: Requiring ISPs to block access to websites and online content that are considered immoral.
4. Reducing Access to Public Libraries: Limiting the availability of books, movies, and media that don't align with morality standards.
5. Censoring Online Streaming Platforms: Forcing streaming services to remove content that violates moral guidelines.
6. Limiting the Availability of Independent Bookstores: Reducing support for independent retailers that offer diverse 'amoral' literature.
7. Restricting Attendance at Live Performances: Imposing regulations that limit who can attend concerts, plays, and other live events.
8. Censoring Content in Video Games: Restricting the themes and narratives allowed in video game production and distribution.
9. Eliminating Funding for Community Arts Programs: Reducing access to local arts initiatives and diverse cultural experiences.
10. Mandating Content Warnings: Requiring content creators to issue warnings for topics deemed controversial or sensitive, potentially discouraging viewership.

Legislating Morality

1. Passing Morality Laws that Govern Content Creation: Legislating what can and cannot be depicted in entertainment based on morality.
2. Imposing Blasphemy Laws on Media: Criminalizing content that is deemed offensive to religious beliefs.
3. Restricting Depictions of Violence and Sex: Enforcing strict limits on the portrayal of violence and sexual content, pornography bans.
4. Banning Satirical or Irreverent Content: Prohibiting content that uses satire or humor to critique societal norms or authorities.
5. Mandating Family-Friendly Content Standards: Requiring that all public media adhere to family-friendly guidelines and religious laws.
6. Censoring Political Commentary: Restricting the ability of artists and media outlets to critique government policies and actions.
7. Imposing Religious Standards on Entertainment: Requiring that all content aligns with the moral teachings of dominant religious groups.
8. Enforcing Decency Standards in Public Performances: Regulating the content of performances to ensure they align with morality laws.
9. Criminalizing the Production and Distribution of Certain Content: Making it illegal to create content that violates new moral laws.
10. Mandating Content Labels Based on Moral Criteria: Requiring content to be labeled according to its adherence to specific moral standards, which could stigmatize and limit its distribution.

Family

Project 2025 and Republican's policies significantly harm families by increasing financial strain, limiting access to quality education and healthcare, and imposing restrictive moral legislation. These actions undermine family stability and well-being, ultimately narrowing the scope of opportunities and support available to diverse family structures across the country.

Economic Strain
1. Cuts to Social Safety Nets: Reducing support for programs like food assistance, housing subsidies, and unemployment benefits, putting financial strain on families.
2. Reducing Access to Affordable Healthcare: Eliminating protections under the Affordable Care Act, leading to higher medical costs.
3. Eliminating Child Tax Credits: Increasing the financial burden on families with children by removing tax relief.
4. Reducing Minimum Wage Protections: Keeping wages low, making it harder for families to make ends meet.
5. Eliminating Paid Family Leave: Forcing families to choose between income and caring for a newborn or sick family member.
6. Cutting Funding for Childcare Assistance: Making quality childcare unaffordable for many families, particularly lower income.
7. Reducing Support for Elder Care Programs: Increasing the financial and emotional strain on families caring for aging relatives.
8. Limiting Access to Affordable Housing: Reducing the availability of affordable housing, leading to housing instability for families.
9. Eliminating Funding for Job Training Programs: Making it harder for parents to gain the skills needed to secure better-paying jobs.
10. Raising Taxes on Middle- and Lower-Income Families: Increasing the tax burden on working families while providing tax cuts to the wealthy.

Education and Child Development
1. Defunding Public Education: Reducing the quality of education available to children, especially in low-income areas.
2. Cutting Early Childhood Education Programs: Limiting access to preschool education, which is crucial for child development.
3. Eliminating After-School Programs: Removing safe, structured environments that support learning and development.
4. Censorship of Educational Content: Restricting the teaching of

49

important subjects like science, history, and social studies.
5. Reducing Funding for Special Education: Making it harder for children with disabilities to receive the support they need.
6. Cutting School Nutrition Programs: Increasing food insecurity among children by reducing access to free or cheaper meals at school.
7. Eliminating Support for Arts and Music Programs: Depriving children of opportunities for creative expression and development.
8. Reducing Funding for School Counseling Services: Limiting access to mental health support for students.
9. Imposing High-Stakes Testing: Creating stress and anxiety for children while narrowing the curriculum to focus on test preparation.
10. Closing Schools in Rural and Low-Income Areas: Forcing families to travel longer distances for education or settle for crowded schools.

Healthcare and Wellbeing
1. Reducing Medicaid Funding: Limiting access to healthcare for low-income families, leading to unmet medical needs.
2. Cutting Mental Health Services: Reducing access to necessary mental health care for children and parents.
3. Eliminating Reproductive Health Services: Removing access to contraception and reproductive healthcare, leading to unplanned pregnancies and financial strain.
4. Reducing Funding for Substance Abuse Programs: Limiting treatment options for families dealing with addiction issues.
5. Cutting Support for Maternal and Child Health Programs: Increasing risks during pregnancy and childbirth, and infant health.
6. Eliminating Support for Family Planning Services: Limiting families' ability to plan and space their children, leading to hardship.
7. Reducing Funding for Vaccination Programs: Increasing the risk of preventable diseases within families.
8. Cutting Nutrition Assistance Programs: Reducing access to healthy food, leading to poor health outcomes for children.
9. Eliminating Support for Home Visiting Programs: Reducing resources that help at-risk families improve parenting skills, outcomes.
10. Weakening Workplace Safety Regulations: Increasing the risk of injury and illness for working parents, affecting family stability.

Family Rights and Social Policies
1. Restricting LGBTQ+ Family Rights: Denying same-sex couples the right to marry, adopt, or access family benefits.
2. Imposing Strict Morality Laws on Family Life: Legislating how

families should live according to specific moral or religious beliefs.
3. Reducing Legal Protections for Women and Children: Weakening laws that protect against domestic violence and child abuse.
4. Cutting Funding for Domestic Violence Shelters: Leaving victims of domestic violence with fewer options for safety and support.
5. Eliminating No-Fault Divorce: Outlawing individuals right to leave unhealthy or abusive marriages.
6. Eliminating Support for Single Parents: Reducing benefits and support programs specifically designed for single-parent families.
7. Censoring Family-Related Content in Media: Limiting the representation of diverse family structures in media entertainment.
8. Weakening Protections for Immigrant Families: Increasing the risk of family separation through deportation and other immigration.
9. Mandating Religious-Based Curriculum in Schools: Forcing all students to adhere to a specific religious ideology, family's beliefs.
10. Opposing Paid Family Leave Policies: Preventing families from taking necessary time off to care for newborns or sick relatives.

Cultural and Community Impact
1. Defunding Community Centers and Social Services: Reducing access to spaces that provide essential services, support for families.
2. Eliminating Support for Community Arts Programs: Reducing opportunities for families to engage in cultural and artistic activities.
3. Cutting Funding for Libraries and Public Spaces: Limiting access to resources and safe spaces for family activities and learning.
4. Restricting Access to Public Parks and Recreation Areas: Reducing the availability of outdoor spaces where families can congregate.
5. Limiting Public Transportation Options: Making it harder for families without cars to access work, school, and social services.
6. Imposing Restrictions on Community Gatherings: Limiting the ability of families to participate in public events and celebrations.
7. Censoring Family-Friendly Media: Removing or altering content that doesn't fit specific moral standards, limiting family options.
8. Reducing Support for Youth Sports Programs: Cutting programs that provide physical activity and opportunities for children.
9. Weakening Environmental Protections: Allowing pollution and environmental degradation that negatively impacts family health.
10. Promoting Segregation in Housing and Schools: Reinforcing social divisions that isolate families from diverse communities.

Finance

The policies of Project 2025 and Republican's eliminate regulatory safeguards in the financial sector, including cryptocurrency markets, leading to increase risks of fraud, market instability, and corporate abuse. By weakening consumer protections and accountability, these changes prioritize short-term profits and interests of the rich vs. long-term financial stability and the well-being of everyday consumers.

Deregulation of Financial Markets
1. Repealing Dodd-Frank Act Provisions: Removing protections put in place after the 2008 financial crisis, increasing the risk of a crash.
2. Eliminating the Volcker Rule: Allowing banks to engage in risky trading activities with depositors' money.
3. Reducing Oversight of Derivatives Trading: Making it easier for financial institutions to trade complex and risky financial products.
4. Weakening Capital Requirements for Banks: Allowing banks to operate with lower capital reserves, increasing financial shocks.
5. Reducing Transparency in Financial Transactions: Decreasing the amount of information that must be disclosed in financial dealings, making it harder to spot fraud.
6. Deregulating the Mortgage Industry: Rolling back rules that prevent predatory lending practices, putting homeowners at risk.
7. Weakening Consumer Protections in Financial Products: Allowing the sale of financial products that are not in the interest of consumers.
8. Limiting the Power of the Securities and Exchange Commission (SEC): Reducing the SEC's ability to regulate and enforce laws against financial misconduct.
9. Removing Restrictions on High-Frequency Trading: Increasing the likelihood of market manipulation and flash crashes.
10. Defunding Financial Regulatory Agencies: Cutting the budgets of agencies that oversee financial markets, reducing risk enforcement.

Corporate Governance and Accountability
1. Reducing Shareholder Rights: Limiting the ability of shareholders to influence corporate governance and hold executives accountable.
2. Weakening Executive Compensation Regulations: Allowing excessive executive pay without ties to company performance.
3. Removing Restrictions on Stock Buybacks: Enabling companies to artificially inflate their stock prices with continued stock manipulation.
4. Decreasing Board of Directors' Accountability: Making it easier for

corporate boards to ignore shareholder concerns.
5. Reducing Transparency in Corporate Reporting: Allowing companies to obscure their financial health and risk from investors.
6. Eliminating Protections for Whistleblowers: Discouraging the reporting of corporate fraud and misconduct.
7. Weakening Insider Trading Laws: Making it easier for executives to profit from non-public information.
8. Reducing Penalties for Corporate Misconduct: Lowering fines and penalties for companies that violate laws and regulations.
9. Allowing Conflicts of Interest in Corporate Governance: Reducing rules that prevent conflicts of interest among corporate leaders.
10. Eliminating Corporate Social Responsibility Requirements: Removing incentives for companies to engage in ethical practices.

Consumer Financial Protections
1. Abolishing the Consumer Financial Protection Bureau (CFPB): Removing the primary federal agency responsible for protecting consumers from financial abuses.
2. Weakening Credit Card and Loan Regulations: Allowing financial institutions to increase fees and interest rates with less oversight.
3. Eliminating Payday Lending Restrictions: Enabling predatory lenders to exploit consumers with high-interest, short-term loans.
4. Reducing Protections Against Identity Theft: Making it easier for criminals to steal and misuse personal financial information.
5. Cutting Funding for Financial Education Programs: Leaving consumers less informed about their financial rights and options.
6. Allowing Discriminatory Lending Practices: Weakening rules that prevent lending discrimination based on race, gender, or income.
7. Reducing Oversight of Debt Collection Practices: Permitting more aggressive and abusive tactics by debt collectors.
8. Weakening Bankruptcy Protections for Individuals: Making it harder for individuals to discharge debt through bankruptcy.
9. Eliminating Restrictions on Adjustable-Rate Mortgages: Allowing lenders to offer high-risk mortgage products leading to foreclosure.
10. Allowing Forced Arbitration Clauses in Financial Contracts: Preventing consumers from taking legal action against institutions.

Tax Policy and Corporate Finance
1. Lowering Corporate Tax Rates: Reducing taxes for corporations, increasing the deficit and shifting the tax burden to individuals.
2. Expanding Tax Loopholes for Multinational Corporations:

Allowing companies to avoid U.S. taxes by shifting profits offshore.
3. Reducing Taxes on Capital Gains: Benefiting the wealthiest individuals who earn most of their income from investments.
4. Allowing Unlimited Corporate Campaign Contributions: Increasing the influence of money in politics, favoring the wealthy.
5. Reducing Transparency in Corporate Tax Filings: Making it harder to track corporate tax avoidance and enforce tax laws.
6. Eliminating the Estate Tax: Allowing wealthy families to pass on large fortunes without paying taxes, exacerbating wealth inequality.
7. Weakening Transfer Pricing Rules: Enabling multinational companies to manipulate prices to minimize tax liabilities.
8. Expanding Deductions for Executive Compensation: Allowing companies to write off excessive executive pay as a business expense.
9. Reducing IRS Enforcement Capabilities: Limiting the ability of the IRS to audit and enforce tax laws, leading to more tax evasion.
10. Allowing More Tax-Free Corporate Mergers and Acquisitions: Encouraging consolidation and reducing competition in the market.

Environmental and Social Governance (ESG) Regulations

1. Eliminating ESG Disclosure Requirements: Allowing companies to hide their environmental, social, and practices from investors.
2. Weakening Climate Risk Reporting: Reducing transparency about how companies are exposed to and addressing climate risks.
3. Reducing Support for Sustainable Investing: Making it harder for investors to choose funds that prioritize ESG factors.
4. Abolishing Green Bond Incentives: Discouraging investment in environmentally sustainable projects.
5. Allowing Increased Pollution without Penalties: Removing fines and sanctions for companies that exceed pollution limits.
6. Weakening Worker Safety Regulations: Increasing the risk of workplace accidents and injuries by reducing safety standards.
7. Eliminating Corporate Diversity Requirements: Allowing companies to ignore diversity and inclusion in their hiring.
8. Reducing Accountability for Human Rights Violations: Allowing companies to engage in practices that violate human rights.
9. Abolishing Renewable Energy Incentives for Corporations: Reducing the adoption of clean energy practices by large companies.
10. Weakening Protections for Local Communities: Allowing companies to bypass local environmental and social regulations.

Government

These categories and examples highlight the destructive impact that Project 2025 and Republican's policies will have on the integrity and functionality of government institutions by eroding democratic norms, promoting corruption, and dismantling essential public services. These actions weaken the government's ability to serve the public, maintain national security, and uphold individual rights, leading to a less effective and more divisive system of governance.

Erosion of Democratic Institutions
1. Undermining the Independence of the Judiciary: Appointing loyalists to the courts, compromising checks on executive power.
2. Weakening Legislative Oversight: Limiting Congress's ability to oversee and hold the executive branch accountable.
3. Gerrymandering Electoral Districts: Redrawing districts to entrench political power and reduce electoral competitiveness.
4. Suppressing Voter Participation: Implementing laws and policies that make it harder for certain groups to vote.
5. Undermining Free Press: Attacking the media, restricting press freedom, and reducing the public's access to unbiased information.
6. Limiting Public Access to Government Information: Reducing transparency and accountability by withholding public information.
7. Politicizing Federal Agencies: Appointing political loyalists to lead nonpartisan federal agencies, undermining their objectivity.
8. Weakening Civil Liberties: Enacting laws that infringe on freedoms of speech, assembly, and protest.
9. Reducing Funding for Independent Oversight Bodies: Cutting budgets for agencies like the Government Accountability Office (GAO) that monitor government actions.
10. Manipulating Census Data: Altering census practices to undercount certain populations, affecting resource allocation.

Corruption and Nepotism
1. Allowing Conflicts of Interest: Permitting government officials to engage in activities that benefit their private interests.
2. Reducing Ethics Rules for Public Officials: Weakening or eliminating ethics regulations preventing corruption, abuse of power.
3. Granting Favorable Contracts to Allies: Awarding government contracts to political supporters without proper bidding processes.
4. Increasing Lobbyist Influence: Allowing lobbyists greater access to

lawmakers, leading to policies that favor special interests over the public good.
5. Encouraging Nepotism in Government Hiring: Allowing the hiring of family members and close associates in key government positions.
6. Undermining Whistleblower Protections: Making it harder for government employees to report unethical or illegal activities.
7. Promoting Regulatory Capture: Allowing industry insiders to regulate the industries from which they came, leading to bias.
8. Reducing Transparency in Government Spending: Obscuring how government funds are allocated and spent, facilitating misuse.
9. Limiting Investigations into Government Misconduct: Reducing the power and reach of bodies tasked with investigating corruption.
10. Eliminating Campaign Finance Regulations: Allowing unlimited contributions to political campaigns, increasing legal bribery.

Dismantling Public Services
1. Cutting Funding for Social Programs: Reducing resources for essential services like healthcare, education, and housing.
2. Privatizing Public Services: Transferring public services to private companies, often leading to higher costs and reduced quality.
3. Reducing Support for Public Infrastructure: Cutting funding for transportation, utilities, and other critical infrastructure projects.
4. Weakening Environmental Protections: Rolling back regulations that safeguard public health and the environment.
5. Eliminating Public Health Initiatives: Reducing funding for disease prevention, emergency preparedness, and other public health services.
6. Decreasing Funding for Education: Undermining public schools by diverting funds to private and charter schools.
7. Cutting Research and Development Funding: Reducing investment in scientific research and technological innovation.
8. Undermining Social Security and Medicare: Proposing cuts to programs that provide financial support to millions of Americans.
9. Reducing Public Sector Jobs: Cutting government jobs, leading to a loss of essential services and expertise.
10. Weakening Labor Protections: Rolling back worker protections, reducing wages, and worsening conditions for public employees.

National Security and Foreign Policy
1. Weakening International Alliances: Undermining relationships with traditional allies, leading to a loss of global influence, security.
2. Reducing Intelligence Capabilities: Cutting funding and resources

for intelligence agencies, hampering their ability to address threats.
3. Politicizing Military Leadership: Appointing loyalists to key military positions, undermining the nonpartisan nature of the armed forces.
4. Undermining Diplomacy: Reducing the role of diplomacy in foreign policy, leading to increased tensions and conflicts.
5. Cutting Foreign Aid: Reducing support for global development and humanitarian programs, weakening U.S. soft power.
6. Neglecting Cybersecurity: Failing to invest in cybersecurity measures, leaving critical infrastructure vulnerable to attacks.
7. Promoting Isolationist Policies: Withdrawing from international agreements and organizations, reducing global cooperation.
8. Reducing Defense Oversight: Limiting Congressional and public oversight of military and defense spending.
9. Weakening Nonproliferation Efforts: Reducing efforts to prevent the spread of nuclear weapons and weapons of mass destruction.
10. Expanding Surveillance Powers: Increasing government surveillance on citizens, infringing on privacy rights.

Legislating Morality
1. Imposing Religious-Based Laws: Enacting laws based on specific religious beliefs, infringing on the separation of church and state.
2. Restricting Reproductive Rights: Implementing policies that limit access to contraception and abortion services.
3. Banning Certain Forms of Expression: Enacting laws that restrict freedom of speech and expression, for marginalized groups.
4. Mandating Religious Education in Public Schools: Requiring the teaching of religious doctrine in public schools.
5. Enforcing Traditional Family Values: Passing laws that restrict the rights of LGBTQ+ individuals and non-traditional families.
6. Censoring Media and Entertainment: Imposing restrictions on what can be broadcast or published based on religious criteria.
7. Criminalizing Personal Behaviors: Enacting laws that criminalize consensual adult behaviors, same-sex relationships or sex work.
8. Restricting Access to Gender-Affirming Care: Banning or limiting healthcare services for transgender individuals.
9. Limiting Academic Freedom: Restricting the ability of educators and researchers to explore and teach certain topics.
10. Legislating Morality-Based Healthcare Decisions: Allowing healthcare providers to deny services based on religious objections.

Health

These categories illustrate the extensive ways in which Project 2025 and Republican's policies severely harm public health by reducing access to healthcare, cutting vital public health initiatives, and weakening environmental protections. These cruel actions will immediately affect vulnerable populations, exacerbate health disparities, and undermine the overall well-being of the nation.

Access to Healthcare
1. Repealing the Affordable Care Act: Eliminating healthcare coverage for millions of Americans, particularly those with pre-existing conditions.
2. Reducing Medicaid Funding: Cutting funds for low-income individuals, leading to decreased access to essential health services.
3. Defunding Planned Parenthood: Removing access to reproductive health services, including cancer screenings and contraception.
4. Weakening Medicare: Cutting benefits and increasing out-of-pocket costs for seniors, making healthcare less affordable for adults.
5. Restricting Access to Reproductive Health Services: Imposing limitations on abortion and contraception, endangering women.
6. Eliminating Protections for Pre-Existing Conditions: Allowing insurers to deny coverage or charge higher rates to those with issues.
7. Reducing Funding for Community Health Centers: Limiting access to primary care services in underserved areas.
8. Eliminating Essential Health Benefits: Ending coverage for essential services like maternity care, mental health, and prescription drugs.
9. Cutting Funding for Mental Health Services: Reducing access to treatment for mental health conditions, leading to worse outcomes.
10. Restricting Access to Substance Abuse Treatment: Limiting availability of treatment programs for those struggling with addiction.

Public Health Initiatives
1. Cutting Funding for Disease Prevention Programs: Reducing resources for programs that prevent the spread of infectious diseases.
2. Defunding Vaccination Programs: Decreasing vaccination rates, leading to the resurgence of preventable diseases.
3. Weakening Environmental Health Protections: Increasing exposure to pollutants contributing to respiratory and cardiovascular diseases.
4. Eliminating Support for Health Education Programs: Reducing public awareness and knowledge of health issues and preventive care.

5. Reducing Funding for Emergency Preparedness: Limiting the ability of public health systems to respond to disasters and pandemics.
6. Dismantling the Centers for Disease Control and Prevention (CDC): Reducing the capacity to track and respond to health crises.
7. Weakening Food Safety Regulations: Increasing the risk of foodborne illnesses by reducing inspections and safety standards.
8. Eliminating Anti-Smoking Programs: Rolling back efforts to reduce smoking rates and prevent tobacco-related illnesses.
9. Reducing Funding for HIV/AIDS Programs: Limiting prevention and treatment efforts, particularly in vulnerable populations.
10. Cutting Support for Maternal and Child Health Programs: Increasing risks during pregnancy and early childhood, leading to higher infant and maternal mortality rates.

Mental Health and Substance Abuse
1. Cutting Funding for Mental Health Services: Reducing access to treatment and support for individuals with mental health conditions.
2. Eliminating Support for Suicide Prevention Programs: Increasing the risk of suicide by reducing public awareness and resources.
3. Reducing Access to Behavioral Health Services: Limiting coverage for therapy, counseling, and psychiatric care.
4. Weakening Opioid Crisis Response Efforts: Cutting funding for programs designed to combat the opioid epidemic.
5. Reducing Support for Substance Abuse Treatment: Limiting the availability of rehabilitation and recovery programs.
6. Eliminating Funding for Community Mental Health Centers: Reducing access to local mental health services.
7. Weakening Workplace Mental Health Protections: Removing requirements for employers to provide mental health support.
8. Defunding School-Based Mental Health Programs: Limiting access to counseling and mental health support for students.
9. Reducing Funding for Veterans' Mental Health Services: Decreasing support for veterans dealing with PTSD and health issues.
10. Cutting Research Funding for Mental Health: Slowing progress in understanding mental health by reducing scientific research funding.

Environmental Health
1. Weakening Clean Air Act Regulations: Allowing more air pollution, which exacerbates respiratory conditions asthma, COPD.
2. Reducing Clean Water Protections: Increasing the risk of contaminated drinking water, leading to health problems like lead

poisoning and gastrointestinal diseases.
3. Rolling Back Climate Change Initiatives: Increasing the frequency of extreme weather events, injury, death, and mental health stress.
4. Allowing Increased Use of Pesticides: Exposing the public to chemicals that are linked to cancer and other health issues.
5. Eliminating Protections for Toxic Waste Sites: Allowing hazardous waste to remain in communities, increasing cancer, birth defect rates.
6. Reducing Oversight of Industrial Pollutants: Allowing industries to release more harmful chemicals into the environment and water.
7. Weakening Protections Against Fracking Pollution: Increasing exposure to harmful chemicals and contaminated water fracking sites.
8. Reducing Regulations on Factory Farming: Increasing the spread of antibiotic-resistant bacteria and environmental degradation.
9. Eliminating Funding for Renewable Energy Programs: Slowing the transition to cleaner energy sources, prolonging exposure to pollution.
10. Cutting Funding for Environmental Research: Limiting our understanding of how environmental factors affect public health.

Health Equity
1. Reducing Funding for Healthcare in Underserved Communities: Increasing health disparities by limiting access to care in rural areas.
2. Eliminating Support for Minority Health Programs: Reducing targeted efforts to address health disparities in minority populations.
3. Weakening Women's Health Programs: Cutting services to women's health needs, including maternal care and cancer screenings.
4. Reducing Support for Immigrant Health Services: Limiting access to healthcare for immigrants, increasing untreated health conditions.
5. Defunding LGBTQ+ Health Initiatives: Removing support for programs that address the health needs of LGBTQ+ individuals.
6. Cutting Funding for Disability Health Services: Reducing access to healthcare for individuals with disabilities, leading to poorer health.
7. Reducing Funding for Elder Care Programs: Limiting healthcare and support services for seniors, increasing their health issues.
8. Weakening Protections Against Healthcare Discrimination: Allowing refusal of treatment based on personal/religious beliefs.
9. Reducing Funding for Telehealth Services: Limiting access in remote or underserved areas who rely on telemedicine.
10. Eliminating Funding for Community Health Workers: Reducing the ability of local health workers to provide culturally competent care in underserved communities.

Housing

Project 2025 and Republican's policies would significantly harm housing access, quality, and affordability across the United States, particularly for low-income and vulnerable populations. By weakening regulations and cutting essential funding, these actions exacerbate housing instability, reduce community development, and deepen social and economic inequalities.

Affordable Housing Access
1. Cutting Funding for Public Housing: Reducing the availability of affordable housing for low-income families.
2. Eliminating Housing Vouchers: Limiting financial assistance for families struggling to afford rent.
3. Reducing Support for First-Time Homebuyer Programs: Making it harder for low- and middle-income families to purchase homes.
4. Weakening Fair Housing Laws: Allowing discriminatory practices in housing markets, making it difficult for minorities to find housing.
5. Defunding Affordable Housing Development: Reducing the construction of new affordable housing units.
6. Eliminating Rent Control Protections: Allowing rents to skyrocket, pushing out low-income tenants.
7. Reducing Funding for Homelessness Prevention Programs: Increasing the risk of homelessness for vulnerable populations.
8. Cutting Support for Rural Housing Programs: Limiting access to affordable housing in rural areas.
9. Reducing Funding for Senior Housing: Making it harder for elderly individuals to find affordable, accessible housing.
10. Weakening Tenant Protections: Making it easier for landlords to evict tenants without just cause.

Housing Quality and Safety
1. Rolling Back Environmental Protections in Housing: Allowing more pollutants in and around residential areas, affecting indoor air quality and health.
2. Weakening Building Safety Codes: Reducing standards for new construction, leading to unsafe housing.
3. Eliminating Lead Abatement Programs: Increasing the risk of lead poisoning in older homes.
4. Cutting Funding for Housing Inspections: Reducing oversight of housing quality, leading to deteriorating living conditions.

5. Reducing Support for Energy Efficiency Upgrades: Making it harder for homeowners and renters to afford energy improvements.
6. Defunding Mold Remediation Programs: Allowing mold problems in homes to go untreated, harming residents' health.
7. Allowing Substandard Housing: Reducing enforcement of housing standards, increasing the prevalence of unsafe, unhealthy homes.
8. Cutting Support for Weatherization Programs: Making homes less resilient to extreme weather conditions.
9. Weakening Asbestos Regulations: Increasing the risk of asbestos exposure in older homes, leading to health issues.
10. Reducing Access to Clean Water in Housing: Allowing water quality to deteriorate in residential areas, leading to health risks.

Homeownership and Financial Stability
1. Reducing Mortgage Interest Deduction: Making homeownership less financially attractive for middle-class families.
2. Weakening Consumer Protections in Mortgage Lending: Allowing predatory lending practices that increase the risk of foreclosure.
3. Eliminating Support for Down Payment Assistance Programs: Making it harder for first-time homebuyers.
4. Increasing Property Taxes Without Offsetting Relief: Burdening homeowners, particularly those on fixed incomes.
5. Cutting Funding for Foreclosure Prevention Programs: Increasing the risk of foreclosure for struggling homeowners.
6. Reducing Access to Low-Interest Loans for Home Improvements: Making it more difficult for homeowners to maintain or upgrade.
7. Weakening Credit Access for Homebuyers: Tightening credit requirements, making it harder for low- and moderate-income families to qualify for mortgages.
8. Reducing Support for Affordable Mortgage Products: Limiting options for affordable home financing.
9. Eliminating Tax Benefits for Homeownership: Making renting more financially attractive than buying, reducing homeownership.
10. Allowing Increases in Adjustable-Rate Mortgages: Exposing homeowners to significant financial risk if interest rates rise.

Community and Urban Development
1. Cutting Funding for Community Development Block Grants (CDBG): Reducing resources for urban renewal and housing.
2. Eliminating Support for Mixed-Income Housing Projects: Limiting the development of communities with diverse income levels.

3. Reducing Funding for Public Transportation: Making it harder for low-income families to access affordable housing near transit options.
4. Defunding Urban Redevelopment Programs: Allowing blighted areas to deteriorate further, reducing housing quality and safety.
5. Reducing Support for Green Spaces in Urban Areas: Limiting the development of parks and recreational areas.
6. Cutting Support for Neighborhood Revitalization Projects: Reducing investments in improving distressed urban neighborhoods.
7. Eliminating Federal Support for Zoning Reform: Preventing the development of affordable housing in high-opportunity areas.
8. Reducing Support for Disaster Resilience in Housing: Leaving homes vulnerable to natural disasters without adequate preparation.
9. Defunding Historic Preservation Programs: Allowing historic neighborhoods to fall into disrepair, reducing their housing stock.
10. Reducing Investment in Affordable Housing Near Jobs: Limiting the development of housing in areas with high employment opportunities, increasing commute times and housing costs.

Social and Economic Equity in Housing
1. Weakening Fair Housing Act Enforcement: Allowing discriminatory housing practices to go unchecked.
2. Reducing Support for Housing Counseling Services: Limiting resources that help families navigate homebuying and renting.
3. Eliminating Affordable Housing Set-Asides: Reducing the number of affordable units in new developments.
4. Weakening Protections for Low-Income Renters: Allowing landlords to increase rents and reduce services for tenants.
5. Cutting Funding for Housing Assistance for Veterans: Increasing homelessness and housing instability among veterans.
6. Reducing Transitional Housing Programs: Limiting resources for individuals transitioning out of homelessness or domestic violence.
7. Allowing Discrimination in Housing Based on Source of Income: Permitting landlords to refuse tenants who rely on housing vouchers.
8. Cutting Programs that Address Housing Discrimination: Reducing efforts to combat redlining and other discriminatory practices.
9. Reducing Support for Rural Housing Initiatives: Leaving rural communities with fewer options for affordable and quality housing.
10. Eliminating Funding for Native American Housing Programs: Neglecting the housing needs of Indigenous communities, leading to overcrowding and poor living conditions.

Immigration

These categories and examples highlight the extensive and detrimental impact that Project 2025 and Republican's policies will have on immigration policies that will severely restrict legal pathways, increase enforcement and deportations, and undermine protections for vulnerable populations. These actions create a hostile environment for immigrants, leading to widespread fear, family separations, and a breakdown in the social fabric of immigrant communities.

Family Separation and Detention
1. Reinstating Family Separation Policies: Forcing the separation of children from their parents at the border, causing trauma.
2. Expanding Detention Facilities: Increasing the number of immigrants held in detention centers, often in inhumane conditions.
3. Reducing Protections for Unaccompanied Minors: Limiting legal protections for children arriving at the border without their parents.
4. Increasing Deportations of Parents with U.S. Citizen Children: Creating fear and instability for mixed-status families.
5. Denying Asylum Seekers Due Process: Fast-tracking deportations without adequate legal representation or hearings.
6. Eliminating Protections for Immigrant Victims of Domestic Violence: Removing the ability to seek asylum for those fleeing abuse.
7. Criminalizing Border Crossings: Treating all unauthorized crossings as criminal offenses, leading to more family separations.
8. Weakening the Flores Settlement Agreement: Allowing longer detentions of children and families, contrary to established norms.
9. Reducing Legal Aid for Detained Immigrants: Limiting access to legal assistance for families in detention, increasing separations.
10. Increasing ICE Raids on Homes and Workplaces: Causing fear and panic in immigrant communities, resulting in family separations.

Restricting Asylum and Refugee Programs
1. Narrowing Asylum Criteria: Limiting the grounds on which individuals can seek asylum, excluding those fleeing gang violence, domestic abuse, and persecution.
2. Capping Refugee Admissions: Drastically reducing the number of refugees allowed to resettle in the United States.
3. Eliminating Temporary Protected Status (TPS): Ending protections for individuals from countries experiencing conflict or disaster.

4. Closing Off Ports of Entry: Making it harder for asylum seekers to present themselves at the border, leading to dangerous crossings.
5. Implementing "Safe Third Country" Agreements: Forcing asylum seekers to apply for protection in countries that may be unsafe.
6. Reducing Legal Aid for Asylum Seekers: Limiting access to legal representation, making it more difficult for asylum seekers.
7. Implementing "Remain in Mexico" Policies: Forcing asylum seekers to wait in Mexico for their U.S. court dates.
8. Speeding Up Asylum Hearings: Reducing the time asylum seekers have to prepare their cases, leading to more denials and deportations.
9. Denying Work Permits to Asylum Seekers: Prohibiting asylum seekers from working legally while their cases are pending.
10. Cutting Funding for Refugee Resettlement Programs: Reducing resources for housing, education, and integration services for refugees.

Hindering Legal Immigration Pathways
1. Eliminating the Diversity Visa Lottery: Reducing immigration from underrepresented countries, particularly in Africa and Asia.
2. Capping Family-Based Immigration: Limiting the ability of U.S. citizens and permanent residents to sponsor relatives for immigration.
3. Increasing Fees for Immigration Applications: Making it more expensive to apply for visas, green cards, and citizenship.
4. Prolonging Green Card Backlogs: Increasing wait times for legal permanent residence, causing uncertainty and stress for applicants.
5. Restricting H-1B and Other Work Visas: Limiting the number of skilled workers allowed to enter the U.S.
6. Ending Birthright Citizenship: Proposing constitutional amendments or laws to deny citizenship to immigrant born births.
7. Reducing Protections for DACA Recipients: Rolling back protections for Dreamers and stripping work permits.
8. Imposing Public Charge Rules: Denying green cards and visas to immigrants deemed likely to use public benefits.
9. Eliminating Parole in Place for Military Families: Ending protections of family of U.S. military personnel to stay in the country.
10. Increasing Denials of Immigration Applications: Arbitrarily denying visa and green card applications, without clear justification.

Criminalization and Enforcement
1. Expanding the 287(g) Program: Allowing local law enforcement to enforce federal immigration laws, leading to racial profiling.
2. Increasing Workplace Immigration Raids: Targeting businesses

that employ undocumented workers, resulting in mass arrests.
3. Implementing Mandatory E-Verify: Requiring all employers to check the immigration status of new hires, leading to job losses.
4. Enhancing Interior Enforcement Operations: Increasing ICE activity within U.S. borders, targeting immigrant communities.
5. Increasing Surveillance of Immigrant Communities: Expanding the use of surveillance technologies to monitor and track immigrants.
6. Expanding the Use of Private Detention Centers: Increasing the number of immigrants held in for-profit detention facilities.
7. Imposing Harsh Penalties for Document Fraud: Increasing criminal penalties for immigrants using false documents.
8. Proposing Federal Charges for Sanctuary Cities: Punishing cities that refuse to cooperate with federal immigration enforcement.
9. Expanding the Definition of "Criminal Alien": Broadening the criteria for deportation based on criminal activity.
10. Reducing Prosecutorial Discretion: Limiting the ability of immigration judges and prosecutors to prioritize cases.

Impact on Immigrant Communities

1. Creating a Climate of Fear: Increasing immigration enforcement and raids, leading to fear and anxiety in immigrant communities.
2. Weakening Protections for Immigrant Workers: Reducing labor protections, leading to exploitation and unsafe working conditions.
3. Eliminating Access to Healthcare for Undocumented Immigrants: Cutting off healthcare options, leading to public health risks.
4. Restricting Access to Education for Undocumented Students: Limiting educational opportunities for children and young adults.
5. Reducing Access to Public Services for Immigrants: Limiting eligibility for social services, increasing poverty and hardship.
6. Encouraging Discrimination in Housing: Allowing landlords to deny housing based on immigration status, leading to homelessness.
7. Limiting Access to Legal Representation: Reducing funding for legal aid programs that assist immigrants, leading deportations.
8. Cutting Support for Immigrant Integration Programs: Reducing resources for language classes, job training, and other services.
9. Restricting Immigrant Access to Driver's Licenses: Making it harder for undocumented immigrants to obtain driver's licenses.
10. Weakening Protections Against Hate Crimes: Reducing enforcement of hate crime laws, leading to increased violence and discrimination against immigrant communities.

International

Project 2025 and Republican's policies weaken U.S. influence abroad by undermining diplomatic relationships, reducing participation in global security efforts, and promoting economic and environmental instability. These actions damage international cooperation, increase global tensions, economic inequality, and the likelihood of conflict.

Diplomatic Relations

1. Withdrawing from International Agreements: Damaging trust with global partners by reneging on treaties and commitments.
2. Undermining Alliances: Weakening traditional alliances, such as NATO, by reducing support and collaboration.
3. Cutting Foreign Aid: Reducing assistance to developing countries, leading to instability and loss of U.S. influence.
4. Promoting Nationalist Policies: Encouraging similar nationalist movements in other countries, increasing global tensions.
5. Reducing Diplomatic Staff and Funding: Closing embassies and consulates, diminishing the U.S.'s presence and influence abroad.
6. Imposing Unilateral Sanctions: Straining relations with allies who oppose such measures, leading to diplomatic rifts.
7. Rejecting Multilateralism: Opposing multilateral institutions like the United Nations, reducing international cooperation.
8. Encouraging Isolationism: Promoting policies that discourage global engagement, leaving a vacuum for other powers to fill.
9. Undermining Climate Agreements: Weakening global climate action by withdrawing from environmental accords.
10. Souring Relations with Emerging Powers: Alienating potential allies in regions like Africa and Latin America through aggressive or dismissive policies.

Global Security

1. Weakening Nonproliferation Efforts: Reducing efforts to prevent the spread of nuclear weapons, other weapons of mass destruction.
2. Cutting Defense Alliances: Reducing commitments to defend allies, emboldening adversaries and increasing global instability.
3. Undermining Counterterrorism Cooperation: Diminishing collaboration with other nations in fighting terrorism.
4. Reducing Cybersecurity Collaboration: Limiting international cooperation on cybersecurity, making global networks vulnerable.
5. Withdrawing from Peacekeeping Missions: Reducing U.S.

involvement in UN and other peacekeeping efforts, aiding conflicts.
6. Supporting Authoritarian Regimes: Bolstering undemocratic governments, leading to human rights abuses and regional instability.
7. Expanding Arms Sales to Conflict Zones: Increasing the proliferation of weapons in unstable regions, exacerbating conflicts.
8. Cutting Support for International Law Enforcement: Reducing cooperation to combat organized crime and human trafficking.
9. Ignoring Global Health Threats: Reducing participation in global health initiatives, increasing the spread of diseases.
10. Undermining Humanitarian Interventions: Opposing international efforts to protect civilians in conflict zones.

Trade and Economy
1. Imposing Tariffs on Allies: Straining economic relationships with traditional trading partners, leading to retaliatory measures.
2. Withdrawing from Trade Agreements: Reducing access to international markets for U.S. businesses, harming economic growth.
3. Promoting Protectionism: Encouraging other countries to adopt protectionist policies, reducing global trade.
4. Cutting Funding for Global Development Projects: Reducing U.S. involvement in global infrastructure and economic development, losing influence on other powers like China.
5. Weakening International Financial Institutions: Undermining institutions like the IMF and World Bank, leading to instability.
6. Encouraging Currency Wars: Promoting competitive devaluations that can lead to global financial instability.
7. Reducing Investment in Emerging Markets: Limiting investment in developing economies, reducing growth and increasing inequality.
8. Withdrawing from Climate-Related Trade Initiatives: Reducing participation in global efforts to promote sustainable trade.
9. Imposing Sanctions Without Allied Support: Damaging the global economy and weakening alliances by unilaterally imposing sanctions.
10. Increasing Economic Inequality: Promoting policies that exacerbate global wealth disparities, leading to social unrest.

Human Rights and Global Governance
1. Undermining Human Rights Initiatives: Reducing support for global human rights organizations, allowing abuses to go unchecked.
2. Weakening the International Criminal Court: Opposing the ICC and its ability to prosecute war crimes and crimes against humanity.
3. Reducing Funding for Humanitarian Aid: Cutting support for

global aid programs, leading to increased suffering in conflict zones.
4. Opposing Gender Equality Initiatives: Reducing U.S. support for global efforts to promote gender equality and women's rights.
5. Supporting Repressive Regimes: Providing aid and arms to governments that violate human rights, worsening abuses.
6. Weakening Refugee Protections: Reducing support for international refugee programs, leaving vulnerable populations at risk.
7. Undermining Global Health Initiatives: Reducing participation that fights diseases like HIV/AIDS, malaria, and COVID-19.
8. Opposing Environmental Protections: Reducing support for international environmental treaties, leading to increased global pollution and climate change.
9. Limiting Freedom of the Press: Supporting regimes that suppress independent journalism, reducing global freedom of expression.
10. Cutting Cultural Exchange Programs: Reducing programs that promote understanding and cooperation between nations.

Climate and Environmental Impact
1. Withdrawing from the Paris Agreement: Reducing global efforts to combat climate change by undermining key international agreements.
2. Cutting Funding for Global Environmental Initiatives: Reducing support for projects that protect biodiversity and combat degradation.
3. Promoting Fossil Fuel Use Internationally: Encouraging other nations to invest in coal and oil, increasing global carbon emissions.
4. Weakening Support for Renewable Energy Development: Limiting global progress in adopting clean energy technologies.
5. Undermining Global Conservation Efforts: Reducing support for protecting endangered species and critical habitats.
6. Opposing International Climate Adaptation Programs: Leaving nations without the resources to cope with climate change.
7. Cutting Contributions to the Green Climate Fund: Reducing financial support for nations to mitigate and adapt to climate change.
8. Increasing Environmental Degradation Through Trade: Promoting trade policies that encourage deforestation and resource extraction.
9. Reducing Support for Ocean Conservation: Weakening efforts to protect marine environments from overfishing and pollution.
10. Encouraging Water Privatization: Supporting the privatization of water resources in developing countries, leading to water scarcity.

Justice

Project 2025 and Republican's policies undermine the justice system by eroding judicial independence, curtailing civil liberties, and exacerbating racial and social injustices. These actions not only weaken the rule of law but also reduce access to justice and increase corruption, leading to a less fair and less accountable legal system.

Undermining Judicial Independence
1. Appointing Partisan Judges: Installing judges who prioritize political loyalty over impartiality, undermining systemic fairness.
2. Reducing Judicial Review: Limiting the courts' ability to review and overturn unconstitutional laws and executive actions.
3. Increasing Political Pressure on Judges: Encouraging politicians to influence judicial decisions, eroding public trust in the judiciary.
4. Limiting the Power of the Supreme Court: Proposing measures that restrict the Supreme Court's ability to check the government.
5. Undermining Judicial Appointments Process: Speeding up confirmations without thorough vetting, leading to biased judges.
6. Defunding Judicial Branch: Cutting funding for courts, leading to longer case backlogs and reduced access to justice.
7. Encouraging "Court Packing": Adding judges to the courts to tilt decisions in favor of specific political outcomes.
8. Politicizing Lower Courts: Appointing judges to lower courts based on their political affiliations rather than legal expertise.
9. Undermining Precedent (Stare Decisis): Encouraging judges to disregard established precedents, creating legal uncertainty.
10. Reducing Transparency in Judicial Processes: Limiting public access to court proceedings and decisions, reducing accountability.

Erosion of Civil Liberties
1. Weakening Protections for Freedom of Speech: Enacting laws that criminalize dissent and restrict free expression.
2. Expanding Surveillance Powers: Increasing government surveillance on citizens without adequate oversight, hurting privacy.
3. Limiting Freedom of Assembly: Imposing restrictions on protests and public gatherings, curbing the right to peaceful assembly.
4. Criminalizing Peaceful Protests: Introducing harsh penalties for participating in protests, deterring civic engagement.
5. Weakening Protections Against Unlawful Search and Seizure: Eroding Fourth Amendment protections by expanding police powers.

6. Reducing Access to Legal Representation: Cutting funding for public defenders and legal aid, making fair trials harder to enable.
7. Restricting Voting Rights: Imposing barriers to voting, disproportionately affecting minorities and other marginalized groups.
8. Expanding Qualified Immunity: Increasing protections for law enforcement officers from civil lawsuits, even in cases of misconduct.
9. Increasing Use of Secret Courts: Utilizing secretive judicial processes, such as FISA courts, without accountability.
10. Restricting Press Freedom: Imposing restrictions on journalists, limiting their ability to report on government activities.

Racial and Social Injustice
1. Expanding Mass Incarceration: Increasing penalties for minor offenses, leading to higher incarceration rates, among minorities.
2. Eliminating Bail Reform Efforts: Maintaining or increasing cash bail requirements, disproportionately affecting low-income and minority defendants.
3. Encouraging Racial Profiling: Allowing law enforcement to target individuals based on race or ethnicity, leading to discrimination.
4. Weakening Hate Crime Protections: Reducing penalties for hate crimes, diminishing legal recourse for victims of racial violence.
5. Undermining Police Accountability: Limiting the ability of communities to hold law enforcement accountable for misconduct.
6. Defunding Community Policing Programs: Reducing support for initiatives that build trust between police and communities of color.
7. Criminalizing Poverty: Enacting laws that disproportionately punish the poor, such as fines for minor infractions and jail time.
8. Undermining Civil Rights Protections: Rolling back protections against discrimination in housing, employment, and education.
9. Expanding Private Prisons: Increasing reliance on private prisons, which profit from higher incarceration rates and often provide inadequate conditions.
10. Restricting Immigrant Rights: Imposing harsh penalties and detentions for immigrants, including those seeking asylum.

Curtailing Access to Justice
1. Cutting Funding for Public Defenders: Reducing the number of public defenders, increasing caseloads and reducing defense quality.
2. Increasing Court Fees and Fines: Making it more expensive to access the court system, particularly for low-income individuals.
3. Limiting Class Action Lawsuits: Making it harder for groups of

people to collectively sue for justice, reducing accountability.
4. Reducing Access to Courts for Civil Rights Cases: Imposing stricter requirements for filing civil rights lawsuits, discouraging legal challenges to discrimination.
5. Expanding Forced Arbitration: Requiring individuals to settle disputes through arbitration rather than courts.
6. Weakening Whistleblower Protections: Reducing protections for individuals who expose corruption or illegal activities, discouraging the reporting of wrongdoing.
7. Eliminating Legal Aid Programs: Cutting funding for organizations that provide legal assistance to low-income individuals.
8. Increasing Use of Summary Judgments: Allowing judges to dismiss cases without trial, reducing the opportunity to present their cases.
9. Restricting Access to Appeals: Limiting the right to appeal court decisions, particularly in criminal cases.
10. Defunding Civil Rights Offices: Reducing the resources available to government offices that enforce civil rights laws, less oversight.

Corruption and Abuse of Power
1. Encouraging Political Interference in Investigations: Allowing elected officials to interfere with criminal investigations for self-gain.
2. Weakening Campaign Finance Laws: Reducing transparency in political donations, increasing the influence of money in politics.
3. Allowing Conflicts of Interest in Government: Permitting officials to engage in activities that benefit their personal financial interests.
4. Limiting the Independence of Prosecutors: Politicizing prosecutorial decisions, undermining the fairness of the legal process.
5. Reducing Oversight of Government Agencies: Cutting funding for oversight bodies that monitor government activities.
6. Expanding Executive Power Without Checks: Increasing the president's authority without adequate checks and balances.
7. Undermining Investigative Journalism: Restricting the ability of the press to investigate and report on government corruption.
8. Reducing Transparency in Government Actions: Limiting public access to information about government decisions and policies.
9. Encouraging Nepotism and Cronyism: Allowing individuals to occupy key government positions based on personal connections.
10. Weakening Enforcement of Ethics Rules: Eroding ethical standards for government officials, allowing for greater misconduct.

Labor

These categories and examples highlight the extensive and detrimental impact that Project 2025 and Republican's policies will have on labor protections by weakening workers' rights, eroding workplace safety standards, and reducing wage and benefit security. These actions not only increase job insecurity and workplace inequalities but also diminish the overall quality of life for workers across the nation.

Weakening Workers' Rights
1. Eliminating Collective Bargaining Rights: Reducing the power of unions to negotiate fair wages, benefits, and conditions for workers.
2. Expanding Right-to-Work Laws: Allowing employees to benefit from union negotiations without paying dues, weakening unions.
3. Restricting Union Organizing Activities: Imposing stricter regulations on union activities, making it harder to organize.
4. Reducing Protections for Striking Workers: Making it easier for employers to replace striking workers permanently.
5. Limiting Union Access to Workplaces: Restricting union representatives from meeting with workers on company property.
6. Expanding At-Will Employment: Allowing employers to fire workers without cause, increasing job insecurity.
7. Weakening Worker Protections Under the National Labor Relations Act (NLRA): Rolling back protections that prevent unfair labor practices by employers.
8. Cutting Funding for the National Labor Relations Board (NLRB): Reducing the ability of the NLRB to enforce labor laws.
9. Encouraging the Use of Non-Compete Agreements: Limiting workers' ability to change jobs or start their own businesses by enforcing restrictive contracts.
10. Eliminating Prevailing Wage Laws: Allowing employers to pay workers less than the standard wage for government-funded projects.

Reducing Workplace Safety and Health Protections
1. Rolling Back Occupational Safety and Health Administration (OSHA) Regulations: Reducing safety standards, leading to fatalities.
2. Cutting Funding for OSHA Inspections: Decreasing the number of workplace inspections, increasing unsafe working conditions.
3. Weakening Protections Against Workplace Hazards: Allowing more exposure to dangerous chemicals and unsafe machinery.

4. Reducing Ergonomic Standards: Eliminating regulations that prevent repetitive strain injuries and other musculoskeletal disorders.
5. Limiting Protections Against Workplace Violence: Reducing requirements for employers to prevent violence in the workplace.
6. Weakening Heat Stress Protections: Reducing safeguards for workers exposed to extreme temperatures, leading illness and death.
7. Cutting Funding for Workplace Safety Training Programs: Limiting education and resources for workers to learn safety practices.
8. Reducing Protections for Temporary and Gig Workers: Allowing companies to evade safety regulations.
9. Allowing Longer Working Hours Without Overtime Pay: Increasing the risk of fatigue-related accidents by ending protections.
10. Weakening Whistleblower Protections: Making it harder for workers to report unsafe conditions without fear of retaliation.

Undermining Wage Protections
1. Eliminating the Federal Minimum Wage: Allowing states to set their own wage floors, potentially lowering wages in many areas.
2. Reducing Overtime Pay Requirements: Allowing more workers to be classified as exempt from overtime, reducing overall earnings.
3. Weakening Equal Pay Protections: Making it harder for workers to challenge pay discrimination based on gender, race, or other factors.
4. Expanding the Use of Wage Theft: Reducing penalties for employers who illegally withhold wages from workers.
5. Allowing Misclassification of Workers: Permitting companies to classify employees as independent contractors, denying benefits.
6. Reducing the Scope of the Fair Labor Standards Act (FLSA): Narrowing the definition of who qualifies for wage protections.
7. Weakening Enforcement of Wage Laws: Cutting funding for agencies that investigate and enforce wage laws.
8. Eliminating Tipped Minimum Wage Protections: Allowing employers to pay tipped workers less than the federal minimum wage.
9. Reducing Transparency in Pay Practices: Allowing companies to hide pay disparities and prevent workers from discussing wages.
10. Weakening Protections for Part-Time Workers: Allowing employers to deny benefits and fair wages to part-time employees.

Eroding Benefits and Job Security
1. Reducing Access to Healthcare Benefits: Allowing employers to cut or reduce health insurance coverage for workers.
2. Eliminating Paid Family and Medical Leave: Denying workers the

right to take paid time off to care for a new child or sick family.
3. Weakening Retirement Security: Reducing protections for pensions and 401(k) plans, leaving workers with less retirement income.
4. Reducing Unemployment Insurance Benefits: Cutting the duration and amount of unemployment benefits, making it harder for workers.
5. Allowing Companies to Reduce Paid Time Off: Permitting employers to eliminate or reduce vacation, sick days, and holidays.
6. Expanding the Use of Temporary Contracts: Encouraging the replacement of full-time employees with temporary or gig workers.
7. Reducing Protections for Disabled Workers: Weakening the Americans with Disabilities Act (ADA) protections.
8. Weakening Protections for Older Workers: Allowing age discrimination in hiring and layoffs, leading to reduced job security.
9. Cutting Support for Job Training and Education Programs: Reducing opportunities for workers to gain new skills and advance.
10. Eliminating Workers' Compensation Protections: Making it harder for injured workers to receive compensation for work injuries.

Exacerbating Inequalities in the Workplace
1. Undermining Anti-Discrimination Laws: Weakening enforcement of laws that protect workers from discrimination.
2. Eliminating Affirmative Action Programs: Reducing efforts to address historical inequalities and promote diversity in the workplace.
3. Weakening Protections for LGBTQ+ Workers: Rolling back protections that prevent discrimination based on sexual orientation.
4. Reducing Support for Pregnant Workers: Weakening protections that ensure fair treatment for pregnant employees.
5. Allowing Religious Exemptions to Workplace Protections: Permitting employers to bypass anti-discrimination laws based on religious beliefs, harming minority groups.
6. Expanding the Gender Pay Gap: Reducing enforcement of equal pay laws, allowing wage disparities to grow.
7. Weakening Language Access Protections: Removing requirements for employers to provide materials and training in multiple languages.
8. Reducing Protections for Immigrant Workers: Allowing employers to exploit immigrant labor by ignoring labor laws and protections.
9. Undermining Disability Rights in Employment: Weakening the requirement for reasonable accommodations, less accessible.
10. Eliminating Support for Workplace Diversity Programs: Cutting funding and support for initiatives that promote inclusion, diversity.

LGBTQ+

Project 2025 and Republican's policies significantly undermine the rights, safety, and well-being of LGBTQ+ individuals by rolling back legal protections, restricting access to healthcare, and promoting discrimination in public and private life. These actions foster a climate of fear and inequality, making it hard to live freely and fully in society.

Legal Rights and Protections
1. Rolling Back Marriage Equality: Attempting to overturn or undermine the legal recognition of same-sex marriages.
2. Eliminating Anti-Discrimination Protections: Allowing discrimination based on sexual orientation and gender identity.
3. Weakening Protections Against Hate Crimes: Reducing penalties and enforcement of laws designed to protect LGBTQ+ individuals.
4. Restricting Access to Legal Gender Changes: Making it more difficult for transgender individuals to change their legal documents.
5. Reversing Non-Discrimination Orders: Revoking executive orders that protect LGBTQ+ federal employees and contractors.
6. Banning LGBTQ+ Representation in Schools: Prohibiting discussions or education about LGBTQ+ issues and history in school.
7. Restricting Parental Rights of LGBTQ+ Individuals: Limiting the ability of LGBTQ+ couples to adopt or foster children.
8. Imposing Religious Exemptions to Anti-Discrimination Laws: Allowing businesses and organizations to refuse service to LGBTQ+.
9. Eliminating Protections in Healthcare: Allowing healthcare providers to refuse treatment to LGBTQ+ patients based on beliefs.
10. Reducing Funding for LGBTQ+ Legal Services: Cutting support for organizations that provide legal assistance to LGBTQ+ persons.

Healthcare Access and Rights
1. Restricting Access to Gender-Affirming Care: Banning or limiting access to medical treatments and surgeries for transgender individuals.
2. Cutting Funding for HIV/AIDS Programs: Reducing support for prevention, treatment, and research efforts targeting LGBTQ+.
3. Allowing Healthcare Discrimination: Permitting healthcare providers to deny care based on sexual orientation or gender identity.
4. Prohibiting Insurance Coverage for Gender-Affirming Treatments: Preventing insurance companies from covering necessary treatments.
5. Eliminating Mental Health Services for LGBTQ+ Individuals:

Cutting funding for counseling and mental health services.
6. Restricting Access to PrEP and Other Preventative Care: Limiting access to medications and services that prevent HIV and STD's.
7. Defunding LGBTQ+ Health Clinics: Reducing support for clinics that provide specialized care to LGBTQ+ communities.
8. Criminalizing Transgender Healthcare Providers: Targeting medical professionals who provide gender-affirming care.
9. Limiting Access to Reproductive Health for LGBTQ+ Individuals: Restricting services like IVF and surrogacy.
10. Banning Conversion Therapy Protections: Allowing the practice of conversion therapy, which is harmful and discredited.

Education and Youth Protection
1. Banning LGBTQ+ Inclusive Curriculum: Prohibiting schools from teaching about LGBTQ+ issues, history, or contributions.
2. Restricting LGBTQ+ Student Organizations: Limiting the formation and operation of Gay-Straight Alliances and other LGBTQ+ student groups.
3. Implementing "Don't Say Gay" Laws: Enforcing laws that prohibit discussions of sexual orientation and gender identity in classrooms.
4. Eliminating Support for LGBTQ+ Students: Reducing funding for school counselors and programs that support LGBTQ+ youth.
5. Promoting Conversion Therapy in Schools: Allowing or encouraging schools to refer students to conversion therapy programs.
6. Banning Transgender Students from Sports: Prohibiting students from playing on sports teams aligning with their gender identity.
7. Allowing Bullying of LGBTQ+ Students: Weakening anti-bullying laws, increased harassment and violence against LGBTQ+ students.
8. Restricting Access to LGBTQ+ Educational Resources: Banning books, websites, and other materials that provide information and support to LGBTQ+ students.
9. Prohibiting LGBTQ+ Topics in Sex Education: Excluding discussions of LGBTQ+ relationships from sex education curricula.
10. Reducing Protections for LGBTQ+ Students in Private Schools: Allowing private schools to discriminate against LGBTQ+ students and staff without losing public funding.

Public and Social Life
1. Censoring LGBTQ+ Content in Media: Imposing restrictions on the portrayal of LGBTQ+ characters and stories in television, movies, and literature.

2. Banning LGBTQ+ Events and Pride Parades: Restricting public gatherings and celebrations of LGBTQ+ culture and identity.
3. Allowing Public Officials to Denounce LGBTQ+ Rights: Encouraging public figures to speak out against LGBTQ+ rights.
4. Restricting LGBTQ+ Participation in Public Service: Discriminating against LGBTQ+ individuals in public service roles.
5. Encouraging Social Media Censorship of LGBTQ+ Content: Pressuring platforms to restrict LGBTQ+ voices online.
6. Limiting Access to LGBTQ+ Friendly Spaces: Reducing funding and support for community centers, shelters, and other safe spaces.
7. Criminalizing Public Displays of LGBTQ+ Identity: Enforcing laws against public expressions of LGBTQ+ identity.
8. Restricting LGBTQ+ Representation in Politics: Implementing policies preventing openly LGBTQ+ to run or hold office.
9. Banning LGBTQ+ Books and Resources in Public Libraries: Removing literature and materials that reflect LGBTQ+ experiences.
10. Allowing Discrimination in Public Accommodations: Permitting businesses and services to refuse LGBTQ+ customers.

Impact on Family and Personal Life
1. Restricting Adoption and Foster Care by LGBTQ+ Couples: Limiting the ability of LGBTQ+ individuals to adopt or foster kids.
2. Undermining Parental Rights of LGBTQ+ Parents: Challenging the legal rights of LGBTQ+ parents to their children.
3. Allowing Discrimination in Family Services: Permitting family service providers, including adoption agencies, to discriminate.
4. Banning Surrogacy and IVF for LGBTQ+ Individuals: Prohibiting access to reproductive technologies that help to start families.
5. Weakening Protections for LGBTQ+ Families in Healthcare: Allowing healthcare providers to deny services to LGBTQ+ families.
6. Criminalizing Same-Sex Intimacy: Reintroducing laws that penalize private consensual relationships between same-sex adults.
7. Restricting LGBTQ+ Family Benefits: Denying LGBTQ+ families access to benefits like health insurance, retirement, and family leave.
8. Targeting LGBTQ+ Elders: Reducing support for LGBTQ+ elderly individuals, including access to culturally competent care.
9. Allowing Religious Exemptions to Deny Services to LGBTQ+ Families: Permitting service providers to refuse services to LGBTQ+.
10. Undermining Estate and Inheritance Rights for LGBTQ+ Couples: Challenging the rights of LGBTQ+ individuals to inherit.

Media

Project 2025 and Republican's policies severely undermine media freedom and integrity by imposing censorship, manipulating economic controls, and promoting propaganda. These actions not only restrict the diversity of information available to the public but also create a climate of fear and self-censorship among journalists, weakening the media's role as a watchdog and pillar of democracy.

Censorship and Content Control
1. Imposing Strict Censorship Laws: Limiting what can be reported or discussed in the media, particularly on controversial or critical topics.
2. Banning Specific Topics from Coverage: Prohibiting the media from covering certain issues, such as government corruption.
3. Implementing "Morality" Guidelines for Content: Requiring media to adhere to specific moral standards, limiting perspective, stories.
4. Restricting Political Commentary: Imposing regulations that limit or censor political analysis and opinions in the media.
5. Enforcing Blasphemy Laws: Banning any media content that is perceived as offensive to religious sensibilities, stifling free expression.
6. Censoring Social Media Platforms: Forcing social media companies to remove content that is deemed inappropriate or sensitive.
7. Banning LGBTQ+ Representation: Prohibiting positive portrayals of LGBTQ+ individuals and issues in the media.
8. Restricting Access to Foreign Media: Limiting the availability of international news and perspectives, creating a more insular media.
9. Mandating Government Approval for Publications: Requiring media outlets to get government clearance before publishing stories, leading to self-censorship.
10. Banning Independent Investigative Journalism: Preventing the media from conducting in-depth investigations that could expose wrongdoing.

Economic Control and Manipulation
1. Cutting Funding for Public Broadcasting: Reducing financial support for public media, leading to decreased coverage of issues.
2. Encouraging Media Monopolies: Allowing a few large corporations to control the majority of media outlets, reducing diversity in news.
3. Imposing Heavy Fines on Non-Compliant Media: Penalizing media outlets that report on stories the government disapproves of.

4. Defunding Independent Media Organizations: Cutting off financial resources for independent and non-profit media outlets.
5. Offering Tax Breaks to Friendly Media: Providing financial incentives to media outlets that align with government views.
6. Restricting Advertising for Certain Media: Limiting the ability of media outlets to attract advertisers, that cover controversial topics.
7. Increasing Licensing Fees for Media Outlets: Making it more expensive to operate a media company, for independent outlets.
8. Promoting State-Controlled Media: Increasing funding for government-run media outlets, crowding out independent voices.
9. Encouraging Corporate Ownership of Media: Acquisition of media outlets by corporations with close government ties, leading to bias.
10. Restricting Foreign Investment in Media: Limiting foreign ownership or influence in domestic media, reducing perspectives.

Attacks on Press Freedom
1. Criminalizing Journalism: Imposing harsh penalties on journalists for reporting on sensitive issues or publishing leaked information.
2. Arresting Journalists: Detaining reporters who investigate or criticize the government, creating a climate of fear.
3. Harassing Media Organizations: Using government agencies to intimidate companies through audits, inspections, and legal threats.
4. Limiting Access to Information: Blocking access to public records, press briefings, and government officials, hindering journalism.
5. Imposing Gag Orders: Preventing media outlets from reporting on specific stories or ongoing investigations.
6. Surveilling Journalists: Monitoring journalists' communications and activities to intimidate them and gather information on their sources.
7. Restricting Freedom of Movement for Journalists: Limiting the ability of reporters to travel to certain countries to cover stories.
8. Increasing Legal Barriers to Press Freedom: Implementing laws that make it easier to sue or prosecute media outlets for defamation.
9. Undermining Whistleblower Protections: Reducing protections for sources who provide information to journalists, discouraging leaks.
10. Promoting Self-Censorship: Encouraging media outlets to avoid controversial topics out of fear of retaliation or legal consequences.

Manipulation of Media Narratives
1. Promoting Propaganda: Using media to disseminate government-approved narratives, drowning out independent and critical voices.
2. Restricting Access to Alternative Media: Limiting public access to

non-mainstream media outlets that provide different perspectives.
3. Encouraging "Fake News" Campaigns: Promoting disinformation to discredit and undermine independent media.
4. Mandating Government Messaging in Media: Requiring media outlets to broadcast government propaganda or announcements.
5. Demonizing the Press: Encouraging public distrust of the media by labeling critical outlets as "enemy of the people" or "fake news."
6. Creating Media Blackouts: Preventing media from reporting on specific events or crises, controlling public perception.
7. Manipulating Social Media Algorithms: Influencing the visibility of certain news stories or perspectives on social media platforms.
8. Limiting Media Pluralism: Reducing the diversity of viewpoints available in the media, leading to a more controlled narrative.
9. Funding Propaganda through State-Owned Media: Expanding state-owned media to spread government-favored narratives globally.
10. Restricting Critical Media from Covering Elections: Limiting the ability of media outlets to report on elections, skewing perception.

Impact on Journalistic Integrity

1. Promoting Conflict of Interest in Media: Allowing media owners to have close ties to political figures, compromising independence.
2. Encouraging Sensationalism Over Substance: Pressuring media to focus on sensational stories that attract attention but lack depth.
3. Reducing Investment in Investigative Journalism: Cutting budgets for in-depth investigations that hold powerful entities accountable.
4. Limiting Editorial Independence: Increasing control over editorial decisions by media owners with political agendas.
5. Promoting Misinformation: Allowing or encouraging the spread of false information through media channels, undermining trust.
6. Discouraging Fact-Checking: Reducing the emphasis on verifying information before publication, leading to the spread of inaccuracies.
7. Pressuring Media to Conform to Government Narratives: Coercing media outlets to align their reporting with government perspectives.
8. Eliminating Ombudsman Roles in Media: Removing internal checks that ensure journalistic standards and integrity.
9. Undermining Public Trust in Media: Encouraging skepticism of all media, leading to confusion and erosion of public knowledge.
10. Encouraging Bias in Reporting: Promoting media coverage that favors certain political, corporate, or ideological interests.

Men

Project 2025 and Republican's policies significantly harm men by undermining their economic stability, health, and family life, while promoting harmful cultural norms. These actions not only reduce men's opportunities for personal and professional growth but also exacerbate social isolation and mental health challenges.

Economic Stability and Employment
1. Weakening Workers' Rights: Reducing collective bargaining and union power, leading to lower wages and fewer benefits for men.
2. Cutting Funding for Job Training Programs: Limiting opportunities for men to acquire new skills and adapt to job markets.
3. Promoting Gig Economy and Temporary Contracts: Encouraging job structures with fewer protections, leading to job insecurity.
4. Reducing Minimum Wage Protections: Allowing wages to stagnate or decrease, making it harder for men to support their families.
5. Weakening Workplace Safety Regulations: Increasing the risk of injuries in male-dominated industries like construction.
6. Cutting Support for Small Businesses: Limiting resources for men who own or wish to start small businesses, reducing opportunities.
7. Reducing Access to Unemployment Benefits: Making it harder for men to receive financial support during periods of joblessness.
8. Eliminating Retirement Security Protections: Weakening pension and 401(k) plans, leading to financial instability for retirement.
9. Expanding Automation Without Worker Retraining: Replacing jobs in manufacturing and other industries with machines.
10. Encouraging Income Inequality: Implementing tax and economic policies that widen the gap between high and low earners.

Health and Wellbeing
1. Reducing Access to Healthcare Services: Cutting funding for Medicaid and other health programs, leading to less options for men.
2. Eliminating Mental Health Support Programs: Reducing access to counseling and mental health services, increasing risk.
3. Weakening Workplace Safety Standards: Increasing the likelihood of occupational injuries and illnesses in male-dominated fields.
4. Reducing Funding for Substance Abuse Programs: Limiting access to treatment for men struggling with addiction.
5. Cutting Funding for Veterans' Health Services: Reducing medical

care options for male veterans, many of whom suffer from PTSD.
6. Weakening Environmental Protections: Increasing exposure to pollutants and toxins that affect men in certain industry.
7. Discouraging Preventive Health Measures: Reducing funding for public health campaigns and services that promote early detection.
8. Allowing Insurers to Deny Coverage Based on Pre-Existing Conditions: Making it harder for men with chronic health conditions.
9. Reducing Support for Rural Healthcare: Limiting access to healthcare in rural areas where many men live and work.
10. Encouraging High-Risk Behaviors: Promoting a culture that discourages seeking help for health issues, leading to increased deaths.

Family and Social Dynamics
1. Weakening Support for Fathers' Rights: Reducing legal protections and support for fathers in custody and child support cases.
2. Cutting Funding for Family Support Services: Limiting access to programs that help men balance work and family responsibilities.
3. Promoting Outdated Gender Roles: Reinforcing stereotypes that limit men's participation in caregiving and domestic roles.
4. Reducing Access to Paternity Leave: Limiting the ability of men to take time off work to care for newborns, affecting family bonding and wellbeing.
5. Encouraging Traditional Masculinity Norms: Promoting cultural expectations that discourage men from expressing emotions.
6. Undermining Educational Support for Boys: Reducing funding for programs that address the unique educational challenges boys face.
7. Cutting Funding for Social Services: Limiting resources for men struggling with homelessness, poverty, and other social issues.
8. Weakening Protections Against Domestic Violence: Reducing support for male victims of domestic violence.
9. Discouraging Male Involvement in Education: Promoting policies that discourage men from pursuing careers in education, childcare.
10. Increasing Divorce Rates Due to Economic Strain: Implementing policies that exacerbate economic instability.

Legal and Justice Systems
1. Reducing Legal Aid for Low-Income Men: Limiting access to legal representation, making it harder for men to defend their rights.
2. Expanding Mass Incarceration: Increasing penalties for minor offenses, leading to higher incarceration rates for men.
3. Encouraging Harsh Sentencing Laws: Promoting policies that

impose long sentences for non-violent crimes.
4. Weakening Rehabilitation Programs in Prisons: Reducing funding for education, job training, and mental health services for men.
5. Limiting Access to Expungement: Making it harder for men with criminal records to clear their names and improve their job prospects.
6. Encouraging the Militarization of Police: Increasing aggressive policing tactics that disproportionately target men.
7. Reducing Support for Reentry Programs: Cutting funding for initiatives that help men transition from prison back into society.
8. Weakening Protections Against Employment Discrimination for Ex-Convicts: Allowing employers to discriminate against men with criminal records, reducing their employment opportunities.
9. Limiting Access to Public Defenders: Reducing funding for public defender offices, leading to overworked attorneys, inadequate defense.
10. Promoting Bias in the Criminal Justice System: Implementing policies that reinforce racial and economic biases.

Social and Cultural Impacts
1. Reinforcing Toxic Masculinity: Promoting cultural norms that encourage aggression and suppress emotional vulnerability in men.
2. Discouraging Men from Seeking Help: Creating a stigma around men accessing mental health services, untreated mental symptoms.
3. Marginalizing Men in Non-Traditional Roles: Discouraging men from pursuing careers outside traditional masculine norms.
4. Promoting Violence as a Masculine Trait: Encouraging a culture that equates masculinity with violence, increased domestic abuse.
5. Discouraging Male Education on Gender Equality: Limiting access to education on gender issues, leading harmful stereotypes.
6. Undermining Male Mentorship Programs: Cutting funding for initiatives that support positive male role models and mentorships.
7. Promoting Alcohol and Substance Use as Coping Mechanisms: Encouraging unhealthy coping strategies for stress, addiction.
8. Reducing Support for Men's Health Initiatives: Limiting public awareness campaigns and services that address men's health issues.
9. Marginalizing LGBTQ+ Men: Promoting policies that discriminate against LGBTQ+ men, leading to increased challenges.
10. Encouraging Isolationism Among Men: Promoting a culture that values self-reliance over community and connection.

Military

These categories and examples highlight the extensive and detrimental impact that Project 2025 and Republicans will have on the military by undermining readiness, morale, and international alliances, while also cutting essential support for military personnel and veterans. These actions not only degrade the effectiveness of the armed forces but also harm the wellbeing of those who serve.

Erosion of Military Readiness
1. Reducing Defense Budgets: Cutting funding for essential military operations, training, and equipment, decreased preparedness.
2. Delaying Modernization Programs: Slowing down the development and procurement of advanced technology and equipment.
3. Reducing Troop Levels: Cutting the number of active-duty personnel, which strains forces and reduces operational capabilities.
4. Cutting Funding for Military Training: Limiting training opportunities, leading to less effective, prepared service members.
5. Defunding Military Infrastructure: Allowing bases and facilities to deteriorate, affecting the living and working conditions of members.
6. Reducing Support for Military Families: Cutting programs that support the families of service members, decreased morale.
7. Cutting Military Healthcare: Reducing access to healthcare services for active-duty members, veterans, and their families.
8. Weakening Support for Veterans: Reducing resources for veterans' programs, leading to gaps in services like mental health care, training.
9. Decreasing Joint Military Exercises: Reducing joint training with allies, weakening international military cooperation and readiness.
10. Defunding Research and Development: Limiting investment in new technologies and innovations maintaining military superiority.

Undermining Military Ethics and Morale
1. Promoting Political Loyalty Over Merit: Appointing military leaders based on political loyalty rather than competence.
2. Weakening Military Justice System: Reducing the effectiveness of military courts in addressing crimes within the ranks.
3. Allowing Discrimination in the Ranks: Rolling back protections against discrimination based on race, gender, and sexual orientation.
4. Encouraging Human Rights Abuses: Promoting policies that disregard international laws and norms, damaging the military's

global reputation.
5. Reducing Support for Mental Health Services: Limiting access to mental health care, leading to higher rates of PTSD and suicide.
6. Promoting Aggressive Policing Tactics: Encouraging the militarization of domestic police forces, which can blur the lines between military and civilian roles.
7. Cutting Diversity and Inclusion Programs: Weakening efforts to create a more inclusive and representative military force.
8. Undermining the Military Code of Conduct: Encouraging behaviors and policies that violate the ethical standards of service.
9. Promoting Authoritarian Leadership Styles: Encouraging a top-down, authoritarian approach to leadership, which can stifle morale.
10. Reducing Respect for Civilian Oversight: Undermining the principle of civilian control over the military, which is fundamental to democracy.

Impact on International Relations
1. Weakening Alliances: Reducing commitments to NATO and other military alliances, leading to increased global instability.
2. Promoting Isolationist Policies: Encouraging a retreat from global engagement, which reduces the military's ability to project power.
3. Undermining International Military Cooperation: Reducing participation in international military exercises and partnerships.
4. Cutting Foreign Military Aid: Reducing support for allied nations' military forces, leading to a decline in global security.
5. Encouraging Unilateral Military Actions: Promoting policies that isolate the U.S. from its allies, increasing the risk of conflict.
6. Withdrawing from International Treaties: Abandoning arms control and defense agreements, leading to a dangerous environment.
7. Reducing Diplomatic Efforts: Limiting the role of diplomacy in conflict resolution, increasing reliance on military force.
8. Encouraging Militarization of Foreign Policy: Prioritizing military solutions over diplomatic ones, leading to prolonged conflicts.
9. Undermining Global Security Partnerships: Weakening cooperative security arrangements to prevent global conflicts.
10. Promoting Arms Races: Encouraging the proliferation of weapons and increasing global tensions through aggressive military posturing.

Impact on Military Personnel and Veterans
1. Reducing Veterans' Benefits: Cutting healthcare, education, and housing benefits for veterans, leading to increased health challenges.

2. Weakening Support for Military Transition Programs: Reducing assistance for service members transitioning to civilian life.
3. Cutting Educational Opportunities for Service Members: Limiting access to GI Bill benefits and other educational programs.
4. Reducing Pay and Compensation: Cutting salaries and benefits for active-duty personnel, leading to lower morale and retention rates.
5. Limiting Access to Mental Health Care: Reducing mental health services for active-duty members and veterans, exacerbating PTSD.
6. Weakening Support for Disabled Veterans: Cutting benefits and services for veterans with disabilities, leading to increased hardship.
7. Undermining Spousal and Family Support Programs: Reducing resources for the spouses and children of military personnel.
8. Increasing Deployment Lengths Without Additional Support: Extending deployment times without providing additional resources.
9. Reducing Housing Allowances: Cutting housing stipends for military families, leading to financial strain and housing insecurity.
10. Undermining Survivor Benefits: Reducing financial support for the families of service members who die in the line of duty.

Erosion of Military Infrastructure and Capability
1. Cutting Funding for Base Maintenance: Allowing military facilities to deteriorate, affecting operational readiness.
2. Delaying Equipment Modernization: Postponing updates to outdated military equipment, leading to reduced effectiveness.
3. Reducing Investment in Cybersecurity: Limiting resources for protecting military networks from cyberattacks, cyber warfare.
4. Weakening the Defense Industrial Base: Reducing support for the industries that supply the military, leading to delays in equipment.
5. Undermining Military Research and Development: Cutting funding for R&D programs that drive innovation and advancement.
6. Reducing Logistics and Supply Chain Support: Limiting the resources needed to maintain global supply lines.
7. Cutting Funding for Military Education and Training Institutions: Weakening the institutions that train military leaders and specialists.
8. Reducing Support for Military Health Facilities: Allowing military hospitals and clinics to decline, affecting the healthcare of members.
9. Limiting Investment in Space and Missile Defense: Reducing funding for programs that protect against new and emerging threats.
10. Encouraging Short-Term Budget Cuts Over Long-Term Strategy: Focusing on immediate cost savings at the expense of readiness.

Minorities

Project 2025 and Republican's policies harm minorities by exacerbating economic inequality, reducing access to education and healthcare, and weakening protections in the criminal justice system. These actions not only limit opportunities for advancement but also deepen systemic disparities, further marginalizing minority communities in every aspect of society.

Economic Inequality
1. Cutting Social Safety Net Programs: Reducing funding for welfare, housing assistance, and food stamps, affecting low-income minorities.
2. Weakening Minimum Wage Protections: Allowing wages to stagnate, making it harder for minority workers to escape poverty.
3. Reducing Access to Affordable Housing: Cutting programs that provide affordable housing, leading to higher rates of homelessness.
4. Limiting Access to Business Loans for Minority-Owned Businesses: Reducing financial support for minority entrepreneurs.
5. Increasing Barriers to Employment: Implementing policies that make it harder for minorities to find and retain jobs.
6. Cutting Funding for Job Training Programs: Reducing access to skills development that are crucial to compete in the job market.
7. Eliminating Affirmative Action: Removing policies that help level the playing field for minorities in education and employment.
8. Weakening Protections Against Wage Discrimination: Making it harder to challenge unequal pay for minorities.
9. Reducing Access to Higher Education: Cutting funding for scholarships and financial aid that support minority students.
10. Promoting Tax Policies that Favor the Wealthy: Implementing tax cuts that benefit high-income earners, widening the wealth gap.

Education and School Segregation
1. Defunding Public Schools in Minority Areas: Reducing resources for schools in predominantly minority communities.
2. Promoting School Vouchers: Diverting funds from public schools to private institutions, exacerbating educational inequalities.
3. Weakening Protections Against Discriminatory Discipline: Harsher punishments for minority students, larger school-to-prison pipeline.
4. Eliminating Bilingual Education Programs: Removing support for students who are English language learners.
5. Promoting Segregation Through Zoning Policies: Encouraging

policies that keep schools racially and economically segregated.
6. Reducing Support for Historically Black Colleges and Universities (HBCUs): Cutting funds for institutions educating minority students.
7. Limiting Access to Advanced Placement (AP) Courses: Reducing opportunities for taking courses that prepare them for college.
8. Eliminating Anti-Bias Training for Teachers: Removing programs that help educators address and reduce racial biases in the classroom.
9. Weakening Protections for LGBTQ+ Students: Allowing discrimination against LGBTQ+ students.
10. Reducing Access to Early Childhood Education: Cutting programs like Head Start, vital for preparing children for school.

Criminal Justice and Policing
1. Expanding Mass Incarceration: Increasing penalties for minor offenses, disproportionately affecting minority communities and exacerbating racial disparities in the criminal justice system.
2. Promoting Aggressive Policing Tactics: Encouraging "tough on crime" policies that lead to over-policing in minority neighborhoods.
3. Weakening Police Accountability: Reducing oversight of law enforcement, more incidents of police brutality against minorities.
4. Eliminating Bail Reform: Maintaining cash bail systems that disproportionately detain minorities who cannot afford to pay for their release.
5. Restricting Voting Rights for Formerly Incarcerated Individuals: Making it harder for people with criminal records, to regain their voting rights.
6. Encouraging Racial Profiling: Allowing law enforcement to target individuals based on race or ethnicity, leading to discrimination.
7. Reducing Access to Public Defenders: Cutting funding for legal defense services, leaving many without adequate representation.
8. Promoting Private Prisons: Expanding the use of private prisons, which profit from higher incarceration rates of minorities.
9. Weakening Juvenile Justice Protections: Treating more juvenile offenders as adults, leading to harsher penalties for minority youth.
10. Increasing Surveillance in Minority Communities: Expanding surveillance programs that target minority neighborhoods.

Health Disparities
1. Cutting Funding for Medicaid: Reducing access to healthcare for low-income minorities who rely on Medicaid for medical services.
2. Reducing Support for Community Health Centers: Closing clinics

that provide essential healthcare services in underserved communities.
3. Weakening Protections for Pre-Existing Conditions: Allowing insurers to deny coverage to individuals with pre-existing conditions.
4. Cutting Funding for Mental Health Services: Reducing access to mental health care, which is already limited in many communities.
5. Promoting Environmental Racism: Allowing pollutants and toxic waste to disproportionately affect minority communities.
6. Reducing Access to Reproductive Health Services: Cutting funding for Planned Parenthood and other providers that offer reproductive health services to minority women.
7. Eliminating Support for HIV/AIDS Prevention Programs: Cutting programs that are crucial for preventing the spread of HIV/AIDS.
8. Reducing Access to Preventive Care: Limiting access to screenings and preventive services that help detect diseases early.
9. Allowing Discrimination in Healthcare: Permitting health providers to refuse patients based on race, ethnicity, or sexual orientation.
10. Cutting Nutrition Assistance Programs: Reducing access to programs like SNAP that help minority families afford healthy food.

Voting Rights and Political Representation

1. Implementing Voter ID Laws: Requiring identification that many minorities do not have, making it harder for them to vote.
2. Gerrymandering to Dilute Minority Votes: Redrawing electoral districts to weaken the political power of minority communities.
3. Purging Voter Rolls: Removing eligible minority voters from registration lists, affecting their ability to participate in elections.
4. Reducing Early Voting and Polling Locations: Limiting access to voting by reducing early voting days and closing polling places.
5. Opposing Automatic Voter Registration: Blocking reforms that would make it easier for minorities to register and vote.
6. Weakening Protections Against Voter Intimidation: Reducing safeguards that protect minority voters from harassment at the polls.
7. Discriminating in Election Administration: Implementing practices that disproportionately burden minority voters.
8. Cutting Funding for Voter Education Programs: Reducing efforts to inform minority communities about their voting rights.
9. Challenging Minority Candidates: Supporting legal and political challenges that make it harder for candidates to run for office.
10. Allowing Discriminatory Redistricting Practices: Permitting the use of racial data in redistricting to undermine communities.

Religion

Project 2025 and Republican's policies harm religious freedom and diversity by promoting state-endorsed religion, undermining religious pluralism, and politicizing religious beliefs. These actions not only marginalize minority faiths but also erode the separation of church and state, leading to a less inclusive and more divided society.

Erosion of Non-Christian Religious Freedom
1. Imposing State-Endorsed Religion: Promoting policies that favor one religion over others, undermining religious freedom.
2. Restricting Religious Practices of Minorities: Implementing laws that limit the ability of minority religions to practice their beliefs.
3. Mandating Religious Observance in Public Schools: Forcing students of all faiths to participate in religious activities.
4. Limiting the Construction of Religious Buildings: Enacting zoning laws that restrict the building of mosques, temples, and synagogues.
5. Restricting Religious Dress: Banning religious garments like hijabs, turbans, or yarmulkes in public spaces, limiting religious expression.
6. Imposing Blasphemy Laws: Criminalizing criticism or questioning of certain religious beliefs, stifling free speech and intellectual inquiry.
7. Limiting Religious Education: Restricting the ability of religious groups to establish and run schools by to their faith-based principles.
8. Reducing Legal Protections for Religious Minorities: Weakening laws that protect minority religions from discrimination.
9. Enforcing Religious Tests for Public Office: Implementing policies that require adherence to a specific religion for holding public office.
10. Limiting Access to Religious Literature: Restricting distribution of religious texts, materials that are not aligned with the dominant faith.

Undermining Religious Pluralism
1. Promoting a Single Religious Narrative in Public Policy: Policies that reflect the values and beliefs of only their chosen "Christianity."
2. Cutting Funding for Interfaith Programs: Reducing support for initiatives that promote dialogue, cooperation between communities.
3. Restricting Religious Representation in Government: Limiting religious leaders from minority faiths in government advisory roles.
4. Banning Multifaith Events: Prohibiting events celebrating multiple religions, discouraging interfaith understanding and cooperation.
5. Undermining Religious Non-Profit Organizations: Reducing

funding and support for religious charities and organizations that do not align with the dominant religion.
6. Promoting Religious Monoculture: Encouraging a cultural and social environment where only one religion is acknowledged.
7. Limiting Religious Media: Restricting the broadcast and publication of religious content that is not from the dominant faith.
8. Opposing Religious Diversity in Schools: Encouraging educational curricula that focus on one religion, misrepresenting others.
9. Discouraging Multifaith Marriages: Promoting policies that make it difficult for individuals of different faiths to marry and raise children according to multiple religious traditions.
10. Weakening Protections Against Religious Discrimination in Employment: Allowing employers to discriminate based on religion.

Politicization of Religion
1. Using Religion as a Political Tool: Exploiting religious beliefs to garner votes, manipulation of religious communities for political gain.
2. Promoting Religious Nationalism: Encouraging a blend of religious and national identity that excludes those of different faiths or beliefs.
3. Mandating Religious-Based Legislation: Passing laws based on specific religious doctrines, undermining a secular legal system.
4. Encouraging Religious Intolerance: Promoting rhetoric that demonizes other religions, fostering division and hostility.
5. Supporting Politically Active Religious Extremists: Providing platforms to extremist groups that promote violence or intolerance.
6. Undermining Separation of Church and State: Blurring the lines between religion and government, leading to policies that favor religious institutions over individual rights.
7. Mandating Prayer in Government Functions: Requiring religious rituals in public government meetings, excluding the non-religious.
8. Promoting Religious Ideologies in Military and Law Enforcement: Encouraging the adoption of religious doctrines in military and police training, potentially leading to bias and discrimination.
9. Imposing Religious Requirements for Public Services: Requiring adherence to certain religious beliefs to receive government benefits.
10. Encouraging Religious-Based Education in Public Schools: Infringing on the rights of students from diverse backgrounds.

Impact on Religious Autonomy
1. Regulating Religious Speech: Imposing restrictions on what religious leaders can preach or teach, limiting religious expression.

2. Interfering in Religious Appointments: Government influence or control in the appointment of religious leaders.
3. Mandating Government Oversight of Religious Institutions: Increasing government control over religious organizations.
4. Enforcing Religious Conformity: Imposing requirements that all religious groups conform to the beliefs of the dominant religion.
5. Limiting Religious Conversions: Restricting the ability of individuals to convert to a different religion.
6. Forcing Religious Institutions to Align with Government Policies: Requiring religious organizations to adopt preapproved policies.
7. Prohibiting Certain Religious Rituals: Banning religious practices that are deemed incompatible with government-approved norms.
8. Regulating Religious Charities and Non-Profits: Imposing burdensome regulations that limit the ability to operate freely.
9. Weakening Legal Protections for Religious Confidentiality: Allowing government access to confidential communications.
10. Controlling Religious Education Content: Mandating government approval of religious educational materials taught by religious schools.

Social and Cultural Marginalization
1. Promoting Stereotypes and Misconceptions: Encouraging negative stereotypes about certain religions, leading to social exclusion.
2. Encouraging Discrimination in Housing: Allowing landlords to refuse housing to individuals based on their religion.
3. Restricting Religious Holidays: Limiting the recognition and observance of religious holidays not part of the dominant faith.
4. Undermining Religious Cultural Practices: Discouraging or banning cultural practices that are tied to specific religious traditions.
5. Fostering Social Divisions Based on Religion: Policies that increase tensions between religious communities, social fragmentation.
6. Encouraging Workplace Discrimination: Allowing employers to discriminate against employees based on their religious beliefs.
7. Reducing Religious Representation in Media: Limiting the portrayal of religious diversity in media, depicting other faiths.
8. Supporting Religious Intolerance in Public Discourse: Promoting public figures who express intolerant views towards certain religions.
9. Discouraging Interfaith Marriage and Relationships: Promoting social norms and policies that stigmatize interfaith relationships.
10. Marginalizing Religious Minorities in Political Representation: Limiting the political representation of minority religious groups.

Taxes

These categories and examples highlight the extensive and detrimental impact that Project 2025 and Republican's policies will have on the tax system by increasing inequality, reducing government revenue, and shifting the tax burden onto middle and low-income individuals. These actions undermine public services, encourage tax evasion, and create a less fair and less effective tax system, ultimately harming the economic stability of the nation.

Increasing Tax Inequality
1. Cutting Taxes for the Wealthy: Implementing tax cuts that benefit the richest individuals, widening the income gap.
2. Reducing Corporate Tax Rates: Allowing corporations to pay less in taxes, shifting the burden onto individuals and small businesses.
3. Eliminating the Estate Tax: Removing taxes on inherited wealth, benefiting the wealthy and exacerbating wealth inequality.
4. Expanding Tax Loopholes for the Rich: Increasing the number of deductions and credits available to high-income earners.
5. Reducing Capital Gains Tax: Lowering taxes on investment income, which primarily benefits wealthy investors.
6. Expanding Offshore Tax Havens: Encouraging the use of offshore accounts to avoid paying U.S. taxes, reducing tax revenue.
7. Allowing Unlimited Deductions for High-Income Earners: Increasing the amount wealthy individuals can deduct.
8. Weakening the Alternative Minimum Tax (AMT): Reducing or eliminating the AMT, ensures high earners pay a minimum tax.
9. Increasing Tax Evasion Opportunities: Reducing IRS enforcement capabilities, making it easier for the wealthy to evade taxes.
10. Promoting Regressive Tax Policies: Shifting more tax burden onto lower-income individuals through sales taxes and fees.

Reducing Government Revenue
1. Implementing Broad-Based Tax Cuts: Cutting income and corporate taxes across the board, reducing government revenue.
2. Eliminating Progressive Tax Brackets: Moving to a flat tax system that reduces taxes for high earners, increasing the burden on the poor.
3. Cutting Excise Taxes: Reducing or eliminating taxes on goods like gasoline and alcohol, which fund important public services.
4. Reducing Import Tariffs: Lowering tariffs on imported goods,

decreasing revenue that supports domestic industries.
5. Expanding Tax Breaks for Corporations: Increasing the number of deductions and credits available to businesses, reducing their tax contributions.
6. Allowing More Tax-Exempt Organizations: Expanding the categories of organizations that can claim tax-exempt status.
7. Weakening IRS Audit Capabilities: Reducing audits of high-income individuals and large corporations, leading to revenue loss.
8. Allowing Tax Avoidance Schemes: Failing to close loopholes for individuals and corporations to avoid paying their fair share of taxes.
9. Reducing Property Taxes: Cutting property taxes, which fund essential local services like education and public safety.
10. Promoting Tax-Free Zones: Creating areas where businesses and individuals can operate without paying taxes, reducing revenue for public services.

Shifting Tax Burden to Middle and Low-Income Individuals

1. Increasing Sales Taxes: Raising sales taxes on lower-income people who spend a larger percentage of their income on essentials.
2. Implementing User Fees: Replacing progressive income taxes with user fees that charge the same amount regardless of income.
3. Reducing Earned Income Tax Credit (EITC): Cutting benefits for working families, increasing their overall tax burden.
4. Weakening Child Tax Credits: Reducing the amount of tax relief available to families with children, increasing financial strain.
5. Increasing Social Security Taxes: Raising payroll taxes, which disproportionately impact low- and middle-income workers.
6. Reducing Deductions for Medical Expenses: Making it harder for individuals to deduct out-of-pocket medical costs.
7. Cutting Education Tax Credits: Eliminating credits for tuition and other education-related expenses, affecting middle-income families.
8. Increasing Taxes on Retirement Savings: Taxing retirement account withdrawals, affecting retirees who rely on these funds.
9. Imposing New Taxes on Essential Services: Introducing taxes on utilities and other essential services, impacting low-income houses.
10. Promoting Regressive Property Tax Reforms: Changing tax assessments in ways that increase the burden on lower-value homes.

Undermining Public Services

1. Cutting Funding for Public Schools: Reducing tax revenue used to fund public education, leading to larger class sizes and resources.

2. Reducing Funding for Infrastructure Projects: Limiting revenue for maintaining and improving roads, bridges, and public transportation.
3. Defunding Social Welfare Programs: Cutting taxes that support programs like food assistance, housing subsidies, and unemployment.
4. Weakening Healthcare Funding: Reducing taxes that fund public health programs and services, leading to less access to care.
5. Cutting Environmental Protection Budgets: Reducing revenue for environmental regulation and conservation efforts.
6. Limiting Funds for Law Enforcement and Public Safety: Reducing tax revenue for police, fire departments, and emergency services.
7. Reducing Support for Veterans: Cutting taxes that fund veterans' healthcare, education, and housing programs.
8. Weakening Public Pension Systems: Reducing funding for public sector pensions, affecting retirees who depend on these benefits.
9. Cutting Arts and Culture Funding: Reducing tax revenue for cultural institutions and public broadcasting.
10. Defunding Disaster Relief Programs: Cutting taxes that fund emergency response and recovery efforts to natural disasters.

Encouraging Corporate and Individual Tax Evasion
1. Reducing IRS Budget and Staffing: Limiting the IRS's ability to audit and enforce tax laws, leading to increased evasion.
2. Promoting Offshore Tax Havens: Allowing corporations and wealthy individuals to hide assets in offshore accounts to avoid taxes.
3. Encouraging Misclassification of Workers: Allowing businesses to classify employees as independent contractors.
4. Weakening Penalties for Tax Evasion: Reducing fines and penalties for individuals and corporations caught evading taxes.
5. Expanding Use of Shell Companies: Encouraging the creation of shell companies to obscure ownership and reduce tax liabilities.
6. Allowing Complex Tax Shelters: Failing to close loopholes that allow the use of complicated financial arrangements to avoid taxes.
7. Reducing Transparency in Corporate Tax Reporting: Making it easier for corporations to underreport income and avoid paying taxes.
8. Encouraging Cash Transactions: Promoting the use of cash to avoid tracking and reporting income to escape taxation.
9. Allowing Exemptions for Large Corporations: Providing specific exemptions that allow businesses to reduce tax obligations unfairly.
10. Weakening International Tax Cooperation: Reducing collaboration with other countries on tax enforcement.

Technology

Project 2025 and Republican's policies harm the technological landscape by stifling innovation, hindering adoption, and exacerbating ethical and privacy concerns. These actions not only slow the pace of technological advancement but also threaten the global competitiveness and security of the U.S. in key emerging sectors like AI, crypto, and CRISPR.

Stifling Innovation
1. Reducing Funding for Research and Development: Cutting support for R&D in AI, CRISPR, and quantum computing.
2. Imposing Restrictive Regulations on AI Development: Implementing regulations that limit deploying AI technologies.
3. Discouraging Public-Private Partnerships: Reducing work between the government and private sector on technological advancements.
4. Banning Certain Applications of CRISPR: Prohibiting the use of gene-editing technologies for ethical or moral reasons.
5. Restricting Access to Blockchain Technology: Imposing regulations that limit the use and development of blockchain.
6. Limiting International Collaboration on Technology: Reducing cooperation with international partners on tech initiatives.
7. Promoting Monopolies in Tech: Mergers and acquisitions that stifle competition and reduce incentives for innovation in the tech sector.
8. Cutting Funding for STEM Education: Reducing investments in science, technology, engineering, and math education.
9. Discouraging Open Source Development: Policies to disincentivize open source contributions, slowing technological innovation.
10. Restricting Data Sharing and Collaboration: Imposing data localization laws that prevent the free flow of information.

Hindering Technological Adoption
1. Imposing High Taxes on Tech Startups: Creating financial barriers for new tech companies, reducing their ability to innovate, compete.
2. Restricting the Use of Cryptocurrencies: Imposing strict regulations on cryptocurrency transactions, limiting integration into the economy.
3. Delaying 5G Network Rollout: Slowing the deployment of next-generation wireless networks, reducing the potential advancements.
4. Blocking AI Integration in Healthcare: Restricting the use of AI in medical diagnostics and treatment planning, hindering advancements.

5. Regulating Autonomous Vehicles Too Harshly: Stringent regulations that slow the development of self-driving cars.
6. Restricting Data Usage for AI Training: Limiting access to large datasets necessary for training AI systems, hampering development.
7. Imposing Limits on CRISPR-Based Agriculture: Banning the use of gene-editing technologies in agriculture, reducing crop yields.
8. Limiting the Use of Blockchain in Supply Chain Management: Restricting blockchain's application in logistics and supply chains.
9. Blocking AI in Public Services: Preventing the use of AI in government services, leading to less effective public administration.
10. Discouraging the Use of AI in Financial Services: Implementing regulations that limit AI's role in financial markets and services.

Ethical and Privacy Concerns
1. Weakening Data Privacy Protections: Rolling back regulations that protect user data, leading to risks of data breaches and misuse by AI.
2. Allowing Unethical Use of AI: Failing to regulate AI applications that violate human rights, in surveillance and biased decision-making.
3. Neglecting Ethical Oversight for CRISPR Technologies: Use of gene-editing technologies without proper ethical review.
4. Permitting Unregulated Use of Facial Recognition: Allowing widespread use of facial recognition technology without proper safeguards, leading to privacy violations.
5. Ignoring Algorithmic Bias in AI: Failing to address biases in AI systems that disproportionately affect marginalized groups.
6. Reducing Transparency in AI Decision-Making: Encouraging the use of AI without requiring explainability, making it difficult to understand and challenge automated decisions.
7. Permitting the Exploitation of Data for Profit: Allowing companies to exploit user data for profit without adequate consent.
8. Neglecting Regulation of Genetic Data: Collection and use of genetic data without strict privacy protections, leading to abuse.
9. Promoting Surveillance Technologies: Development and use of AI-powered surveillance, threatening civil liberties and privacy.
10. Ignoring the Environmental Impact of Tech: Failing to address the environmental costs of technology development and usage.

Economic and Social Disruption
1. Exacerbating Job Displacement Due to AI and Automation: Failing to provide support for workers displaced by automation.
2. Widening the Digital Divide: Reducing investment in digital

infrastructure for underserved communities, exacerbating inequalities.
3. Promoting Unequal Access to Genetic Technologies: Allowing advanced medical technologies to be accessible only to the wealthy.
4. Encouraging Monopolistic Practices in Tech: Allowing tech giants to dominate markets, stifling innovation and consumer choice.
5. Reducing Support for Tech Worker Protections: Weakening labor laws that protect tech workers, leading to exploitation.
6. Undermining Consumer Rights in the Tech Sector: Reducing protections for consumers against deceptive practices.
7. Allowing Unequal Distribution of Technological Benefits: Implementing policies that favor certain regions or groups, leading to uneven economic growth and access to technology.
8. Cutting Support for Retraining Programs: Reducing funding to help workers transition to new roles in a tech-driven economy.
9. Promoting Tech That Displaces Small Businesses: Encouraging the adoption of technologies that only benefit large corporations.
10. Exacerbating Social Isolation Through Technology: Failing to address the social impacts of increased reliance on technology.

Global Competitiveness and Security
1. Reducing Investment in Cybersecurity: Cutting funding for cybersecurity initiatives, leaving critical infrastructure and data.
2. Weakening International Tech Alliances: Reducing collaboration with global partners on technology standards and innovation.
3. Allowing Tech Brain Drain: Implementing policies that drive talent overseas, reducing the domestic tech workforce and capacity.
4. Undermining U.S. Leadership in AI: Cutting support for AI research and development, allowing other nations to surpass in AI.
5. Failing to Regulate Cryptocurrencies Adequately: Creating an unstable environment for cryptocurrencies, market volatility.
6. Weakening Intellectual Property Protections: Allowing intellectual property theft, reducing incentives for innovation in technology.
7. Ignoring the Need for Global AI Ethics Standards: Failing to promote international agreements on AI ethics.
8. Promoting Export Controls on Advanced Technologies: Restricting the export of U.S. tech, reducing global market opportunities.
9. Undermining International Research Collaboration: Reducing opportunities for joint research projects with international partners.
10. Failing to Address Technological Espionage: Allowing foreign entities to steal technological secrets, weakening the U.S.'s edge.

Transportation

Project 2025 and Republican's policies significantly harm the transportation sector by undermining infrastructure investment, exacerbating environmental impact, and increasing economic and social inequalities. These actions not only reduce the safety and reliability of transportation systems but also hinder future innovations that could enhance mobility and sustainability.

Infrastructure Deterioration
1. Cutting Funding for Road Maintenance: Cutting budgets for repairing and maintaining highways and roads.
2. Defunding Bridge Repairs: Allowing aging bridges to fall into disrepair, increasing the risk of accidents and closures.
3. Reducing Investment in Public Transit Systems: Limiting funding for buses, subways, and trains, less reliable and less frequent service.
4. Delaying Upgrades to Traffic Management Systems: Postponing updates to traffic lights and signaling systems, causing congestion.
5. Ignoring Rural Transportation Needs: Failing to invest in transportation infrastructure in rural areas, isolating communities.
6. Cutting Funding for High-Speed Rail Projects: Halting the development of high-speed rail, reducing options for efficient travel.
7. Reducing Support for Urban Transportation Projects: Cutting funds for bike lanes, pedestrian paths, and other urban improvements.
8. Neglecting Ports and Waterways Maintenance: Reducing investment in upgrading ports, harbors, and inland waterways.
9. Defunding Airport Infrastructure Projects: Cutting funds for airport expansions and upgrades, more outdated facilities and congestion.
10. Cutting Support for Electric Vehicle Charging Infrastructure: Limiting the expansion of EV charging stations, halting EV adoption.

Environmental Impact
1. Rolling Back Emissions Standards for Vehicles: Weakening regulations on vehicle emissions, leading to increased air pollution.
2. Defunding Public Transportation Initiatives: Cutting support for transit systems that reduce car usage and lower carbon emissions.
3. Encouraging Fossil Fuel Dependency: Promoting policies that favor gasoline and diesel vehicles over electric and hybrid options.
4. Reducing Investment in Green Transportation: Limiting funding for research and development of sustainable transport technologies.

5. Eliminating Support for Bicycle and Pedestrian Projects: Cutting funding for non-motorized transportation options.
6. Weakening Fuel Efficiency Standards: Allowing automakers to produce less fuel-efficient vehicles, increasing fuel pollution.
7. Promoting Highway Expansion Over Public Transit: Prioritizing highway construction that encourages car use and sprawl.
8. Reducing Protections for National Parks and Public Lands: Allowing infrastructure projects that degrade natural landscapes.
9. Encouraging Urban Sprawl: Promoting policies that lead to suburban expansion, increased reliance on cars, reduced open spaces.
10. Weakening Environmental Impact Assessments: Reducing the requirements for environmental reviews of transportation projects.

Economic and Social Inequality
1. Reducing Access to Affordable Transportation: Cutting funding for subsidized transit fares, making public transportation less accessible.
2. Neglecting Transportation in Underserved Areas: Failing to invest in transit options for low-income and minority neighborhoods.
3. Limiting Funding for Transportation Assistance Programs: Cutting programs that help elderly and disabled individuals access services.
4. Encouraging Toll Roads and Private Highways: Promoting policies that lead to more toll roads, which affect low-income drivers.
5. Reducing Support for School Transportation: Cutting funds for school bus services, making it harder for children in rural and underserved areas to access education.
6. Eliminating Urban Transit Development: Reducing investments in urban transit, leading to gentrification and displacement of residents.
7. Promoting Policies that Favor Car Ownership: Implementing policies that prioritize car ownership, fewer transportation options.
8. Weakening Protections Against Transportation Discrimination: Allowing discrimination in the provision of transportation services.
9. Cutting Support for Rural Transportation Infrastructure: Limiting funds for rural road and bridge maintenance, increasing isolation.
10. Encouraging Privatization of Public Transit: Pushing for the privatization of transit systems, leading to higher fares, fewer services.

Safety and Reliability
1. Reducing Funding for Highway Safety Programs: Cutting support for initiatives that improve road safety, more accidents and fatalities.
2. Defunding Rail Safety Upgrades: Limiting investment in rail infrastructure and safety technologies, increasing the risk of accidents.

3. Weakening Aviation Safety Standards: Reducing oversight and regulation of the aviation industry, compromising passenger safety.
4. Cutting Funding for Traffic Safety Education: Reducing public awareness campaigns that promote safe driving practices.
5. Reducing Support for Emergency Response Services: Limiting funding for services that respond to transportation-related emergencies, increasing response times and risk.
6. Allowing the Use of Unsafe Vehicles on Roads: Weakening regulations that ensure vehicles meet safety standards.
7. Reducing Funding for Vehicle Safety Research: Cutting support for studies and innovations that improve vehicle safety features.
8. Delaying Infrastructure Repairs: Postponing necessary maintenance and repairs on roads and bridges, increasing accidents.
9. Weakening Regulations on Commercial Trucking: Reducing safety standards for the trucking industry, leading to more accidents involving commercial vehicles.
10. Defunding Safety Inspections for Public Transportation: Reducing the frequency and thoroughness of safety inspections.

Innovation and Future Mobility
1. Cutting Support for Autonomous Vehicle Development: Cutting funding for research and testing of self-driving cars, slowing solutions.
2. Limiting Investment in Smart Transportation Systems: Scaling back funding for technologies that improve traffic flow, congestion.
3. Discouraging the Development of Hyperloop and High-Speed Rail: Limiting support that could revolutionize long-distance travel.
4. Reducing Funding for Electric Vehicle Infrastructure: Hindering the development of charging networks and EV adoption technologies.
5. Opposing Investments in Urban Air Mobility: Restricting funding for the development of air taxis and innovative transport solutions.
6. Discouraging Micromobility Solutions: Limiting the integration of bikes, scooters, and small-scale transportation into urban planning.
7. Delaying the Implementation of Vehicle-to-Infrastructure (V2I) Technologies: Postponing the use of infrastructure for safer travel.
8. Cutting Research into Sustainable Aviation: Cutting support for the development of electric or hybrid aircraft, reducing air pollution.
9. Hindering the Deployment of Connected Vehicles: Limiting the rollout of vehicles that communicate, improving safety and efficiency.
10. Opposing Investments in Space Transportation: Cutting funding for initiatives that support commercial spaceflight.

Veterans

These categories and examples highlight the extensive and detrimental impact that Project 2025 and Republican's policies will have on veterans by cutting essential healthcare, economic support, and legal assistance, while also undermining community support systems and long-term care. These actions not only reduce the quality of life for veterans but also break the promises made to those who served the nation, leaving them without the support they deserve.

Healthcare and Mental Health Services
1. Cutting Funding for VA Healthcare: Cutting budgets for Veterans Affairs hospitals and clinics, longer wait times, reduced quality of care.
2. Reducing Access to Mental Health Services: Limiting availability of mental health support for veterans, increasing rates of untreated PTSD and depression.
3. Eliminating Telehealth Programs: Cutting remote healthcare services that are crucial for veterans in rural areas.
4. Weakening Support for Substance Abuse Treatment: Reducing funding for programs that help veterans struggling with addiction.
5. Cutting Funding for Traumatic Brain Injury (TBI) Treatment: Limiting access to specialized care for veterans with TBIs.
6. Reducing Support for Caregiver Programs: Cutting programs that assist family members caring for disabled veterans.
7. Limiting Access to Women's Health Services: Reducing healthcare services tailored to female veterans, a growing segment of the military.
8. Eliminating Funding for Preventive Care: Cutting services that help prevent serious health issues, leading to worse health outcomes.
9. Reducing Funding for Veterans' Dental Care: Limiting access to dental care, which is not universally provided to veterans.
10. Weakening Programs for Homeless Veterans: Cutting funding for initiatives that provide healthcare and shelter to homeless veterans.

Economic and Employment Support
1. Reducing GI Bill Benefits: Cutting education benefits that help veterans transition to civilian careers, limiting their opportunities.
2. Eliminating Veterans' Job Training Programs: Reducing funding for programs that provide veterans with skills needed for civilian jobs.
3. Weakening Support for Veteran-Owned Businesses: Reducing grants and loans available to veterans starting their own businesses.

4. Cutting Employment Assistance Programs: Reducing job placement and career counseling services for veterans.
5. Reducing Funding for Vocational Rehabilitation: Limiting programs that help disabled veterans retrain for new careers.
6. Eliminating Support for Veterans' Housing: Cutting funding for affordable housing programs for veterans, increasing homelessness.
7. Reducing Pension Benefits: Cutting financial support for low-income veterans, leading to increased poverty among aging veterans.
8. Weakening Unemployment Benefits for Veterans: Reducing unemployment insurance or benefits that help veterans.
9. Limiting Access to Apprenticeships and Internships: Reducing programs that provide veterans with on-the-job training.
10. Promoting Privatization of Veterans' Services: Shifting services to private providers who may not understand veterans' unique needs.

Legal and Advocacy Support
1. Reducing Funding for Legal Assistance: Cutting programs that help veterans with legal aid, disability claims, and housing disputes.
2. Weakening Protections Against Employment Discrimination: Reducing enforcement of laws that protect veterans in the workplace.
3. Eliminating Support for Disability Claims Assistance: Limiting access to services that help veterans file and appeal disability claims.
4. Reducing Access to Veterans' Advocacy Groups: Cutting funding for organizations that advocate for veterans' rights and services.
5. Limiting Access to Legal Recourse for Wrongful Discharges: Making it harder for veterans to challenge wrongful discharges.
6. Weakening Support for Veterans' Family Legal Issues: Reducing assistance for legal issues affecting veterans' families.
7. Eliminating Resources for Veterans Facing Foreclosure: Cutting programs that provide legal and financial assistance to veterans.
8. Reducing Support for Immigration Services for Veterans: Limiting access to legal assistance for veterans who are immigrants.
9. Promoting Rollbacks of Civil Rights Protections: Weakening protections that prevent discrimination against veterans in housing.
10. Cutting Funding for Veterans' Rights Education: Limiting programs that educate veterans about their legal rights.

Social and Community Support
1. Cutting Funding for Veterans' Community Centers: Reducing support for places where veterans can connect with peers, services.
2. Eliminating Support for Veterans' Mental Health Peer Support:

Reducing programs that allow veterans to support each other.
3. Reducing Funding for Veterans' Recreation Programs: Cutting services that provide recreational and therapeutic activities.
4. Limiting Access to Veterans' Support Groups: Cutting funding for support groups that help veterans cope with issues like PTSD.
5. Eliminating Veterans' Family Support Programs: Cutting services that help veterans' families cope with the challenges of military life.
6. Reducing Support for Veterans' Cultural and Heritage Programs: Cutting programs that preserve and promote veterans' histories.
7. Eliminating Funding for Veterans' Outreach Services: Reducing initiatives that connect veterans with the services and support.
8. Cutting Support for Veterans' Homelessness Prevention Programs: Cutting funding that prevents veterans from becoming homeless.
9. Reducing Funding for Veterans' Reintegration Programs: Limiting services that help veterans transition back into civilian life.
10. Promoting the Closure of Veterans' Social Services Offices: Closing local offices that provide essential services to veterans.

Retirement and Long-Term Care

1. Reducing Access to Veterans' Long-Term Care Facilities: Cutting funding for nursing homes and other long-term care options.
2. Eliminating Support for Veterans' Home Care Services: Reducing funding for in-home care that helps veterans remain independent.
3. Weakening Pension Plans for Veterans: Reducing the value or availability of pensions for retired veterans.
4. Cutting Funding for Veterans' Hospice Care: Limiting access to end-of-life care services that provide comfort and dignity.
5. Reducing Access to Assisted Living for Veterans: Cutting programs that help veterans afford assisted living facilities.
6. Eliminating Support for Veterans' Aging in Place Programs: Reducing funding for services that help older vets stay in their homes.
7. Weakening Support for Veterans' Spousal Benefits: Reducing financial and healthcare support for the spouses of deceased veterans.
8. Cutting Funding for Veterans' Financial Planning Services: Reducing access to services that help veterans manage their finances.
9. Eliminating Veterans' Retirement Counseling Programs: Cutting programs that help veterans plan for retirement and their benefits.
10. Reducing Access to Geriatric Care for Veterans: Limiting specialized medical care for elderly veterans.

Women

Project 2025 and Republican's policies significantly harm women by stripping away reproductive rights, undermining family and marriage protections, and perpetuating economic and social inequalities. These actions not only restrict women's autonomy and opportunities but also increase their vulnerability to violence and discrimination.

Reproductive Rights and Healthcare
1. Criminalizing Abortion: Implementing laws that ban or severely restrict abortion, putting women's lives and health at risk.
2. Banning Birth Control: Outlawing or limiting access to contraceptives, taking away women's ability to control their reproductive health and plan their families.
3. Eliminating Access to Emergency Contraception: Restricting or banning access to Plan B and other emergency contraceptives.
4. Reducing Funding for Reproductive Health Clinics: Cutting financial support for clinics that provide essential services.
5. Mandating Parental or Spousal Consent for Birth Control: Requiring women to obtain permission from a parent or spouse.
6. Criminalizing Miscarriages: Imposing legal consequences for women who experience miscarriages.
7. Prohibiting In Vitro Fertilization (IVF): Banning or restricting access to fertility treatments like IVF, reducing options for women.
8. Limiting Access to Prenatal and Postnatal Care: Cutting funding for healthcare services that support women during pregnancy.
9. Defunding Planned Parenthood and Similar Organizations: Targeting organizations that provide comprehensive healthcare.
10. Restricting Telemedicine for Reproductive Healthcare: Banning the use of telemedicine for consultations and prescriptions.

Marriage and Family Rights
1. Bringing Back Fault Divorce: Reversing no-fault divorce laws, making it harder for women to leave abusive or unhappy marriages.
2. Limiting Alimony and Child Support: Reducing or eliminating financial support for women after divorce.
3. Promoting Mandatory Marriage Counseling: Requiring couples to undergo counseling before being allowed to divorce.
4. Restricting Custody Rights for Divorced Women: Implementing policies that favor fathers in custody disputes.
5. Encouraging Marriage as the Only Legitimate Family Structure:

Promoting policies that stigmatize single mothers.
6. Undermining Protections for Domestic Violence Survivors: Rolling back legal protections that help women escape abusive marriages.
7. Reducing Access to Legal Representation in Divorce Cases: Cutting funding for legal aid programs that help women.
8. Mandating Joint Custody in All Cases: Imposing joint custody regardless of the circumstances, which can be detrimental.
9. Promoting Policies that Encourage Women to Stay in Marriages: Tax incentives to keep women even in abusive marriages.
10. Reducing Protections Against Marital Rape: Weakening laws that protect women from sexual violence within marriage.

Workplace and Economic Inequality
1. Weakening Equal Pay Laws: Rolling back legislation that ensures women are paid equally for equal work, growing the gender pay gap.
2. Limiting Access to Paid Family Leave: Opposing policies that provide paid leave for new mothers.
3. Reducing Support for Affordable Childcare: Cutting funding for childcare assistance programs, inadequate care options.
4. Promoting Traditional Gender Roles in the Workplace: Encouraging policies that women should prioritize home over career.
5. Eliminating Affirmative Action in Hiring: Removing policies that promote gender diversity in the workplace, reducing opportunities.
6. Reducing Funding for Women's Business Grants and Loans: Cutting financial support for female entrepreneurs.
7. Weakening Protections Against Workplace Harassment: Rolling back regulations that protect women from sexual harassment.
8. Opposing Efforts to Close the Gender Pay Gap: Refusing to support measures that address wage disparities between genders.
9. Reducing Access to Professional Development for Women: Cutting programs that help women advance in their careers through training.
10. Promoting Policies that Undermine Work-Life Balance: Implementing policies that discourage flexible work arrangements.

Education and Social Inequality
1. Defunding Title IX Protections: Weakening the enforcement of Title IX, which protects women and girls from discrimination.
2. Cutting Support for Women in STEM Programs: Cutting funding for women in science, technology, engineering, and math (STEM).
3. Limiting Access to Higher Education for Women: Reducing funding for scholarships and financial aid programs for women.

4. Encouraging Single-Sex Education in Public Schools: Promoting policies that separate boys and girls in public schools.
5. Promoting Abstinence-Only Sex Education: Reducing comprehensive sex education in favor of abstinence-only programs.
6. Reducing Funding for Women's History and Gender Studies: Cutting programs that educate students about women's contributions.
7. Weakening Protections for LGBTQ+ Women in Schools: Reducing support for policies that protect LGBTQ+ women.
8. Promoting Traditional Gender Roles in Education: Encouraging curricula that reinforce traditional gender roles.
9. Cutting Support for Women's Sports Programs: Reducing funding for athletic programs that empower girls and teach leadership skills.
10. Limiting Access to Educational Resources for Women: Reducing funding for libraries, tutoring, and other educational resources.

Violence and Legal Protections
1. Weakening Laws Against Domestic Violence: Rolling back legal protections that help women escape abusive relationships, making it harder to obtain restraining orders or emergency shelter.
2. Reducing Funding for Domestic Violence Shelters: Cutting financial support for shelters that provide safety and resources.
3. Weakening Protections Against Sexual Assault: Rolling back laws that protect women from sexual violence, in the workplace.
4. Reducing Support for Law Enforcement Training on Gender-Based Violence: Limiting funding for programs that train police on how to handle domestic violence and sexual assault cases effectively.
5. Opposing Gun Control Measures: Failing to implement gun control measures reducing domestic violence homicides.
6. Weakening Protections for Immigrant Women: Reducing protections for immigrant women, victims of domestic violence.
7. Reducing Access to Legal Aid for Survivors of Violence: Cutting funding for legal services that help women obtain restraining orders and navigate the legal system after experiencing violence.
8. Limiting Access to Safe Housing for Abuse Survivors: Reducing support for housing programs that help women escape abusive situations and rebuild their lives.
9. Undermining Protections for Trafficking Victims: Reducing efforts to combat human trafficking and support victims.
10. Promoting a Culture of Silence Around Abuse: Encouraging policies and rhetoric that discourage women from speaking out.

Note on Original Sin

The Christo-fascist Republican obsession with the concept of original sin has profoundly shaped their political movements and policies, resulting in a new and overt form of patriarchy that permeates every aspect of their agenda. This ideology, rooted in a fundamentalist interpretation of "Christian" theology, views humanity, particularly women, as inherently flawed and in need of strict moral and social governance. This belief system has become a powerful tool for justifying patriarchal control and has led to the development of policies that systematically undermine the rights and freedoms of women, while reinforcing traditional gender roles.

At the core of Project 2025 and the Christo-fascist Republican ideology is the belief in original sin, the idea that all humans are born sinful due to the fall of Adam and Eve in the Garden of Eden. This doctrine has long been used to justify the subordination of women, who are often seen as the primary bearers of this sin due to Eve's role in the biblical narrative. Within this framework, women are viewed as morally weaker and in need of male guidance and control to maintain societal order. This theological perspective has been co-opted by Christo-fascist Republicans to support a broader political agenda that seeks to reassert male dominance in both the public and private spheres. By framing their policies as necessary for addressing the moral failings of society, they are able to justify patriarchal control as not only a political necessity but a moral imperative.

One of the most direct manifestations of this obsession with original sin is the aggressive assault on reproductive rights. Christo-fascist Republicans have championed policies that seek to criminalize abortion, ban birth control, and restrict access to reproductive healthcare. These policies are rooted in the belief that women, as bearers of original sin, cannot be trusted to make moral decisions about their own bodies. Instead, these decisions must be controlled by the state, guided by patriarchal and religious principles. The criminalization of abortion is particularly telling of this agenda. By making abortion illegal or highly restricted, these policies force women to carry unwanted pregnancies to term, regardless of the circumstances. This not only strips women of their autonomy but also places their health and lives at significant risk. Moreover, it reinforces the notion that women's primary value lies in their ability to reproduce, reducing them to their biological functions rather than recognizing their full humanity. Efforts to ban birth control further erode women's autonomy by removing their ability to prevent unwanted pregnancies. This policy, rooted in the belief that sexual activity should only occur within marriage and for procreation, ignores the realities of modern life and the diverse needs of women. By restricting access to contraceptives, Christo-fascist Republicans seek to control women's sexuality, reinforcing a model where women's bodies are regulated according to patriarchal norms.

The impact of this ideology extends beyond reproductive rights into the realm of gender roles and family structures. Christo-fascist Republicans have promoted policies that seek to reinforce traditional gender roles, often under the guise of protecting family values. These policies include efforts to reintroduce fault-based divorce, reduce support for single mothers, and promote traditional marriage as the only legitimate family structure. By making it more difficult for women to leave marriages without proving fault, these policies trap women in potentially abusive or unfulfilling relationships, reinforcing the idea that their primary role is to serve and obey their husbands. This not only undermines women's autonomy but also perpetuates cycles of abuse and control within the family unit.

Moreover, by promoting traditional marriage and stigmatizing single mothers, Christo-fascist Republicans seek to limit the range of acceptable family structures, ensuring that women remain dependent on male partners for economic and social support. This not only restricts women's choices but also marginalizes those who do not conform to traditional gender roles, further entrenching patriarchal norms. The Christo-fascist obsession with original sin also manifests in economic policies that disproportionately disadvantage women, further entrenching gender inequality. By opposing paid family leave, reducing access to affordable childcare, and weakening workplace protections, these policies make it difficult for women to achieve financial independence and economic security. Paid family leave is a critical policy that allows women to balance work and family responsibilities without sacrificing their careers. By opposing such measures, Christo-fascist Republicans force women to choose between their jobs and their families, often resulting in reduced earning potential and career advancement. This not only limits women's economic opportunities but also reinforces the notion that their primary role is within the home, caring for children and supporting their husbands. The reduction of affordable childcare options further exacerbates this problem by making it financially unfeasible for many women to remain in the workforce. Without access to affordable and reliable childcare, many women are forced to leave their jobs or reduce their working hours, leading to a loss of income and economic security. This perpetuates a cycle of dependence on male partners or the state, undermining women's financial autonomy and freedom.

Weakening workplace protections, such as equal pay laws and anti-discrimination policies, further entrenches economic inequality. By allowing employers to pay women less than men for the same work and by reducing the ability of women to challenge workplace harassment and discrimination, these policies ensure that women remain economically marginalized and vulnerable. This economic disempowerment not only affects individual women but also has broader societal implications, as it limits the overall economic growth and prosperity that comes from a fully inclusive workforce. Education is another area where the Christo-fascist Republican agenda seeks to limit opportunities for women and girls. By defunding Title IX protections and cutting support for women in STEM programs, these policies aim to restrict educational opportunities that empower women to pursue careers and leadership roles dominated by men.

Furthermore, the promotion of abstinence-only sex education, which often accompanies this agenda, leaves girls without critical knowledge about their bodies and health. By focusing exclusively on abstinence and omitting comprehensive information about contraception and sexual health, these programs perpetuate ignorance and stigma around female sexuality. This lack of education not only increases the risk of unintended pregnancies but also reinforces harmful stereotypes that equate female sexuality with sin and shame. These educational policies are part of a broader effort to socialize girls into accepting traditional gender roles from a young age. By limiting their exposure to diverse career paths and reinforcing the idea that their primary value lies in their ability to be wives and mothers, these policies restrict girls' ambitions and opportunities, ensuring that they remain dependent on male authority throughout their lives.

Note on the Two Santa Clause Theory

The "Two Santa Claus Theory," posits that by cutting taxes, Republicans can create a perception of generosity similar to Democrats' spending on social services. However, this approach has been used not only as a political strategy to gain favor but also as a smokescreen to advance a deeper, more troubling agenda. Since the Reagan administration, this theory has provided a cover for policies that increase national debt, slash taxes for the wealthy, erode civil liberties—particularly for women and minorities—and systematically dismantle government social services in favor of privatization.

The implementation of the Two Santa Claus Theory began in earnest during Ronald Reagan's presidency. Reagan's administration championed significant tax cuts, particularly benefiting the wealthy and corporations, under the guise of "trickle-down economics." The idea was that reducing the tax burden on the rich would stimulate investment and economic growth, ultimately benefiting everyone. However, in reality, these tax cuts primarily enriched the already wealthy, while the promised benefits for the broader population failed to materialize. Simultaneously, Reagan's policies led to a dramatic increase in the national debt. This was a calculated move, as the growing debt was then used to justify cuts to social programs. The rationale was that the government could no longer afford to sustain welfare programs, healthcare, and other social services, leading to a gradual erosion of the social safety net.

While the public was distracted by the allure of tax cuts and economic growth promises, a more insidious agenda was being advanced. The Two Santa Claus Theory provided a convenient cover for policies that systematically undermined civil liberties and targeted vulnerable populations, particularly women and minorities. One of the most significant impacts of this strategy has been on women's rights. Under the guise of fiscal conservatism, the government has cut funding for programs that support women, such as Planned Parenthood and other reproductive health services. By framing these cuts as necessary for reducing the deficit, the government obscured its true intent: to control women's bodies and restrict their autonomy.

Minorities have also been disproportionately affected by this agenda. The cuts to social services, such as housing assistance, food stamps, and education funding, have disproportionately impacted minority communities. These communities are often more reliant on government support due to systemic inequalities, and the reduction of these services has deepened the cycle of poverty and marginalization. The Two Santa Claus Theory distracts from these realities by focusing public attention on tax cuts and economic growth, while the erosion of civil liberties and social justice goes largely unnoticed.

The Republican strategy has not only attacked economic and social services but has also led to a significant erosion of civil liberties. In the name of fiscal responsibility and national security, the government has implemented policies that infringe on privacy, freedom of speech, and the right to protest. These measures are often justified by the need to combat crime or terrorism, but in practice, they disproportionately target minority communities and political dissidents. For example, the War on Drugs, initiated under Reagan, has been used as a tool to criminalize and incarcerate large numbers of African Americans and Latinos, stripping them of their civil rights and exacerbating racial inequalities. Similarly, the expansion of surveillance programs and the militarization of the police have created a climate of fear and repression, particularly in minority neighborhoods. Women's rights have also been eroded under this agenda. Beyond the assault on reproductive rights, there has been a concerted effort to roll back protections against workplace discrimination and sexual harassment. These policies are framed as efforts to reduce government regulation and promote business interests, but they effectively strip women of legal protections and recourse, reinforcing patriarchal power structures.

The final prong of the Christo-fascist Republican agenda, as facilitated by the Two Santa Claus Theory, and exemplified in Project 2025 is the systematic gutting of social services in favor of privatization. By creating budget crises through tax cuts and increased debt, the government has manufactured the need to cut public services. These cuts are then used as justification for privatizing essential services, such as healthcare, education, and even social security. Privatization is presented as a more efficient alternative to government-run services, but in reality, leads to higher costs, reduced access, and diminished quality of care. For example, the push to privatize healthcare has resulted in millions of Americans losing access to affordable insurance, while corporate profits in the healthcare industry have soared. Similarly, the privatization of education, through charter schools and voucher programs, has led to segregation and inequality in the school system, as public schools are defunded and left to fail.

The impact on women and minorities has been particularly severe. As social services are cut or privatized, those who are most dependent on these services are left without support. Women, who are often primary caregivers and more likely to rely on services such as childcare and healthcare, are disproportionately affected. Minorities, who face systemic barriers to economic mobility, are further marginalized as the safety net is dismantled. The Christo-fascist Republican obsession with the Two Santa Claus Theory has been a powerful tool for advancing an agenda that systematically undermines civil liberties, cuts taxes for the rich, and dismantles social services. By distracting the public with promises of tax cuts and economic growth, the government has been able to implement policies that reinforce patriarchal control and deepen economic and social inequalities.

The true intent of this agenda is not fiscal responsibility or economic growth but the consolidation of power in the hands of a wealthy, predominantly white, male elite. By cutting taxes for the rich, increasing the debt, and gutting social services, the government has created a society where the most vulnerable are left to fend for themselves, while the wealthy are shielded from the consequences of their policies. The erosion of civil liberties, particularly for women and minorities, is not an unintended consequence but a deliberate strategy to maintain control and suppress dissent. By rolling back protections and rights, the government is ensuring that those who are most affected by their policies are the least able to fight back. The Two Santa Claus Theory is not about providing gifts to the public but about creating a smokescreen for a deeply regressive and authoritarian agenda. It is a strategy that has successfully distracted and divided the public while advancing a vision of society that is fundamentally unequal and unjust.

Note on the GI Bill

The G.I. Bill, officially known as the Servicemen's Readjustment Act of 1944, is often hailed as one of the most significant pieces of social legislation in American history. By providing returning World War II veterans with access to education, housing, and unemployment benefits, the G.I. Bill not only transformed the lives of millions of individuals but also had far-reaching economic and social benefits for the entire country. This landmark legislation demonstrated the profound impact that investment in social programs can have on society, disproving the notion that America is too big for such initiatives or that the country cannot afford them. The argument that there is no money for healthcare, childcare, paid family leave, education, and similar programs is undermined by the fact that there always seems to be ample funding for military spending and wars. This disparity highlights the importance of reevaluating national priorities to ensure that social investment is given the attention and resources it deserves. We can have nice things and pay for it, too.

The G.I. Bill was introduced in response to concerns about the potential economic and social upheaval that could follow the return of millions of veterans after World War II. The legislation provided veterans with benefits that included tuition assistance for higher education, low-cost home loans, and unemployment compensation. The impact of these benefits was profound and far-reaching. Education benefits under the G.I. Bill allowed millions of veterans to attend college or vocational training programs, which they might not have been able to afford otherwise. This influx of educated individuals into the workforce contributed to a significant expansion of the American middle class and helped fuel the economic boom of the post-war era. The benefits of this investment in human capital were not limited to the individuals who received the education; they also extended to the broader economy through increased productivity, innovation, and consumer spending.

The housing benefits provided under the G.I. Bill also had a transformative effect on American society. By making homeownership more accessible to veterans, the bill contributed to the growth of suburban communities and the expansion of the housing market. This not only provided stable living conditions for millions of families but also stimulated economic activity in related industries, such as construction, manufacturing, and retail. Moreover, the unemployment benefits offered by the G.I. Bill provided a safety net for veterans as they transitioned back into civilian life. This financial support helped prevent economic instability and mass unemployment, further contributing to the post-war economic expansion.

The success of the G.I. Bill serves as a compelling argument for the benefits of investing in social programs. When the government invests in the well-being of its citizens, the returns are manifold: individuals are better equipped to contribute to the economy, families are more stable, and social cohesion is strengthened. This is true not only for veterans but for all members of society. Healthcare, childcare, paid family leave, and education are all areas where investment could yield significant social and economic benefits. When people are healthy, they are better able to work, care for their families, and contribute .

Similarly, access to affordable childcare enables parents, particularly women, to participate in the workforce without the burden of unaffordable care options. Paid family leave allows workers to care for their loved ones without sacrificing their financial stability. Both policies not only improve the quality of life for families but also contribute to economic growth by increasing labor force participation and reducing employee turnover. Investment in education is perhaps the most direct way to enhance human capital and ensure long-term economic growth. By providing access to quality education at all levels, the government can equip individuals with the skills and knowledge they need to succeed in a rapidly changing economy. Education is also a powerful tool for reducing inequality and promoting social mobility, ensuring that all individuals have the opportunity to reach their full potential.

Despite the clear benefits of social investment, there is a persistent argument that the United States is too big for such programs or that there is simply no money to fund them. However, this argument falls apart when one considers the vast sums of money that are regularly allocated to military spending and wars. The U.S. defense budget is consistently one of the largest in the world, far outpacing spending on healthcare, education, and social services. This disparity in funding priorities is not a matter of necessity but of choice. The government has demonstrated time and again that it can find the money to fund military operations, often without significant public debate or scrutiny. In contrast, social programs are frequently subjected to intense scrutiny, with their costs portrayed as unaffordable or irresponsible.

The notion that there is no money for social programs is a myth. The real issue is how resources are allocated and what priorities are set by those in power. If the same level of political will and financial commitment that is directed toward military spending were applied to social programs, the benefits for society would be immense. Reallocating even a fraction of the defense budget toward social programs could have a transformative effect on American society. For example, investing in universal healthcare would ensure that all citizens have access to the care they need, reducing healthcare disparities and improving public health outcomes. Similarly, funding universal childcare and paid family leave would support working families, boost labor force participation, and promote gender equality in the workplace.

The G.I. Bill serves as a powerful example of how government investment in social programs can yield significant economic and social benefits. By providing veterans with access to education, housing, and financial support, the G.I. Bill not only transformed the lives of millions of individuals but also contributed to the broader economic prosperity of the post-war era. This success story underscores the potential benefits of investing in social programs for all members of society. The argument that America is too big for such programs or that there is no money to fund them is a myth that obscures the real issue of how national priorities are set. The vast resources allocated to military spending and wars demonstrate that the government has the capacity to fund large-scale initiatives when it chooses to do so. Reallocating resources toward social programs would not only improve the lives of individuals but also strengthen the economy and society as a whole, unlike the gutting in Project 2025.

Investing in healthcare, childcare, paid family leave, and education is not only morally just but also economically prudent. By prioritizing the well-being of its citizens, the government can create a more prosperous, equitable, and resilient society. The success of the G.I. Bill shows that when the government invests in people, the returns are immeasurable, and the impact is felt for generations to come.

Timeline of Money in Politics

Project 2025 is about making ever more money for those at the top. The relationship between money and politics in the United States has evolved significantly over the decades, primarily shaped by a series of Supreme Court rulings that have progressively allowed more financial influence in the political process. This timeline provides an overview of key events and decisions that have marked this evolution, focusing on pivotal moments such as the Powell Memo, the Buckley v. Valeo decision, and Citizens United v. FEC.

The Powell Memo (1971)

- Date: August 23, 1971

- Author: Lewis F. Powell Jr., a corporate lawyer who later became a Supreme Court Justice.

- Overview: The Powell Memo, officially titled "Attack on the American Free Enterprise System," was a confidential memorandum written to the U.S. Chamber of Commerce. Powell argued that the American free enterprise system was under broad attack from leftist groups, academia, and the media. He urged the business community to become more actively involved in shaping public policy, specifically by influencing the intellectual and political climate.

- Impact: The memo is considered a blueprint for the rise of conservative think tanks, lobbying groups, and corporate political action committees (PACs) that would later play a significant role in American politics. It marked the beginning of a more organized and strategic approach by corporations to influence politics and policy.

Federal Election Campaign Act (FECA), Amendments (1971, 1974)

- Date: 1971 (Act passed), 1974 (Amendments added)

- Overview: The FECA was enacted to regulate political campaign spending and fundraising. The 1974 amendments, passed in the wake of the Watergate scandal, imposed stricter limits on contributions to federal campaigns and established the Federal Election Commission (FEC) to enforce campaign finance laws.

- Impact: These regulations were designed to limit the influence of wealthy individuals and special interest groups in elections, though they would later be challenged and weakened by subsequent court rulings.

Buckley v. Valeo (1976)

- Date: January 30, 1976

- Overview: In Buckley v. Valeo, the Supreme Court reviewed the constitutionality of the FECA's provisions. The Court upheld limits on individual contributions to political campaigns but struck down limits on campaign expenditures by candidates and independent expenditures by individuals or groups, arguing that these were protected forms of free speech under the First Amendment.

- Impact: The ruling established the principle that money, as a form of speech, could not be limited in certain contexts. This decision opened the door for increased spending in politics, particularly through independent expenditures, and set the stage for the development of "soft money" contributions to political parties.

First National Bank of Boston v. Bellotti (1978)

- Date: April 26, 1978

- Overview: The Supreme Court ruled that corporations have a First Amendment right to make contributions to influence political processes, such as ballot measures. The decision was based on the idea that speech should not be suppressed simply because it comes from a corporation rather than an individual.

- Impact: This ruling further expanded the role of corporate money in politics, setting a precedent for the protection of corporate political speech and leading to the increased influence of corporations in public policy debates.

Austin v. Michigan Chamber of Commerce (1990)

- Date: March 27, 1990

- Overview: In this case, the Supreme Court upheld a Michigan law that prohibited corporations from using their treasury funds for independent expenditures in support of or opposition to candidates in elections. The Court ruled that this restriction was justified to prevent corruption or the appearance of corruption.

- Impact: This decision was significant because it acknowledged the potential for corporate spending to corrupt the political process. However, it was later overturned by the Citizens United ruling.

Bipartisan Campaign Reform Act (BCRA) - McCain-Feingold Act (2002)

- Date: March 27, 2002

- Overview: The BCRA, commonly known as the McCain-Feingold Act, was passed to address issues that had arisen with campaign finance, particularly the use of "soft money" (unregulated contributions to political parties) and "issue ads" that were designed to influence elections. The Act banned soft money contributions to national political parties and restricted the use of corporate and union money for issue ads in the weeks leading up to elections.

- Impact: The BCRA was a major effort to limit the influence of money in politics, but its key provisions were later challenged and partially invalidated by the Citizens United decision.

Citizens United v. Federal Election Commission (2010)

- Date: January 21, 2010

- Overview: Citizens United, a conservative non-profit organization, sought to air a film critical of Hillary Clinton during the 2008 Democratic primaries. The FEC blocked the film, citing the BCRA's restrictions on corporate-funded electioneering communications.

Citizens United challenged this decision, and the case ultimately reached the Supreme Court. The Court ruled in favor of Citizens United, striking down BCRA's restrictions on independent expenditures by corporations and unions, asserting that such spending is a form of protected speech under the First Amendment.

- Impact: This landmark decision effectively allowed unlimited corporate and union spending on independent political activities, leading to the creation of Super PACs (Political Action Committees) that could raise and spend unlimited amounts of money to influence elections, as long as they did not directly coordinate with candidates. This ruling is often cited as a major factor in the surge of money in politics and the increasing influence of wealthy individuals and special interest groups in the American political system.

Speechnow.org v. FEC (2010)

- Date: March 26, 2010

- Overview: Following the Citizens United decision, the U.S. Court of Appeals for the D.C. Circuit ruled in Speechnow.org v. FEC that contributions to groups that only make independent expenditures (like Super PACs) could not be limited, effectively removing contribution limits to these entities.

- Impact: This ruling further solidified the role of Super PACs in American elections, allowing them to collect and spend unlimited amounts of money from individuals, corporations, and unions. This decision reinforced the influence of money in politics, enabling wealthy donors to have an outsized impact on election outcomes and policy discussions.

McCutcheon v. Federal Election Commission (2014)

- Date: April 2, 2014

- Overview: In McCutcheon v. FEC, the Supreme Court struck down the aggregate limits on how much an individual could donate to federal candidates, political parties, and PACs in a two-year election cycle. The Court ruled that these limits infringed on free speech rights.

- Impact: By removing aggregate limits on contributions, the ruling allowed individuals to donate larger total sums across multiple candidates and political committees, further increasing the influence of wealthy donors in politics.

Present Day Corruption, Partisan Bribes, Lack of Ethics

The timeline of Supreme Court rulings from the Powell Memo to Citizens United and beyond demonstrates a clear trajectory: a steady increase in the role of money in American politics, driven by legal decisions that have expanded the definition of free speech to include monetary contributions and expenditures. These rulings have led to a political landscape where wealthy individuals, corporations, and special interest groups wield significant power, often at the expense of broader democratic participation. As the influence of money in politics continues to grow, concerns about the erosion of democratic principles and the increasing marginalization of ordinary voters have also intensified. The challenge remains to find a balance between protecting free speech and ensuring a political system that is fair, transparent, and accessible to all citizens, regardless of their financial resources, and eliminating the absurd notion corporations are people.

The U.S. Supreme Court has faced growing scrutiny over allegations of corruption and partisan influences, particularly concerning Justices Clarence Thomas, Samuel Alito, and Chief Justice John Roberts. Reports of lavish gifts and undisclosed financial dealings have raised serious concerns about potential bribes and conflicts of interest. These justices have been linked to wealthy conservative donors with business before the court like Harlan Crow, and radical activists like Leonard Leo with extreme right wing political agendas, undermining public trust in the Court's impartiality. The lack of a binding code of ethics for Supreme Court justices exacerbates the issue, as there are no clear consequences for unethical behavior. This absence of accountability threatens the integrity of the judiciary, allowing partisanship and personal gain to erode the principles of justice and fairness that the Court is supposed to uphold. The need for comprehensive ethics reform is critical to restoring faith in the highest court of the land.

Timeline of the Heritage Foundation

The Heritage Foundation, established in 1973, has long been a central figure in shaping conservative policy in the United States. Over the decades, it has wielded significant influence over Republican lawmakers and presidents, from Ronald Reagan to Donald Trump. The organization has consistently pushed a far-right agenda under the guise of preserving American values, often invoking Christian principles to justify its positions. However, a closer examination of the Heritage Foundation's history reveals a pattern of hypocrisy, a dangerous alignment with Christo-fascist ideology, and a set of policies that, if fully implemented, would not only erode the pillars of a free society but also devastate the American economy.

Unoriginal at their core, Project 2025 is any "conservative" or "Christian" fever dream for power. The Heritage Foundation was founded by Paul Weyrich, Edwin Feulner, and Joseph Coors with the intention of providing a conservative counterweight to the liberal think tanks that dominated Washington, D.C., at the time. The organization quickly rose to prominence, particularly during the Reagan administration, when its policy recommendations became the backbone of many of Reagan's economic and social initiatives. The foundation's publication, "Mandate for Leadership," was famously adopted by Reagan's transition team, leading to its significant influence on domestic and foreign policy.

Over the years, the Heritage Foundation has positioned itself as a champion of limited government, free markets, and traditional values. It has advocated for tax cuts, deregulation, and the rollback of social programs, all under the banner of promoting individual freedom and responsibility. However, this ideological stance often masks a more insidious agenda—one that seeks to impose a narrow, "Christian" worldview on the entire country. Despite its professed commitment to freedom and limited government, the Heritage Foundation has frequently supported policies that infringe on individual liberties and promote state intervention in deeply personal matters. This hypocrisy is perhaps most evident in its approach to issues like reproductive rights, LGBTQ+ rights, and religious freedom.

For instance, the Heritage Foundation has been a vocal advocate for overturning Roe v. Wade and restricting access to abortion. This stance is framed as a defense of the sanctity of life, yet it blatantly disregards the autonomy and freedom of women to make decisions about their own bodies. Similarly, the foundation has opposed same-sex marriage and supported so-called "religious freedom" laws that allow businesses to discriminate against LGBTQ+ individuals under the guise of protecting religious beliefs. These positions reveal a troubling double standard: while the Heritage Foundation claims to champion freedom, it is willing to curtail the rights of others to enforce its own moral and religious values.

Moreover, the Heritage Foundation's economic policies are rife with contradictions. The organization has consistently pushed for tax cuts for the wealthy and corporations, arguing that this will spur economic growth and benefit all Americans. However, these policies have instead contributed to growing income inequality and have disproportionately benefited the rich at the expense of the middle and working classes. The foundation's support for deregulation, particularly in the financial sector, played a role in the 2008 financial crisis, further demonstrating the dangers of its economic agenda.

At its core, the Heritage Foundation's agenda is deeply intertwined with a Christo-fascist ideology that seeks to merge Christian nationalism with authoritarian governance. This agenda is evident in the foundation's relentless efforts to shape public policy in ways that reflect its narrow interpretation of "Christian" values, often at the expense of pluralism and democratic principles. The Heritage Foundation has long sought to blur the lines between church and state, advocating for policies that elevate "Christian" beliefs to the level of government policy. This is particularly evident in its education initiatives, where the foundation has pushed for school voucher programs that funnel public money into religious schools, undermining the secular nature of public education. It has also supported efforts to introduce prayer and religious instruction in public schools, further eroding the separation of church and state.

In addition to its domestic agenda, the Heritage Foundation has also promoted a militaristic and interventionist foreign policy that aligns with its Christo-fascist worldview. The foundation has consistently supported aggressive military action and has justified these policies using a moralistic rhetoric that frames the United States as a defender of Christian civilization against perceived threats, both foreign and domestic. This approach not only endangers global stability but also reinforces a dangerous sense of American exceptionalism rooted in religious nationalism.

While the Heritage Foundation's social agenda is deeply concerning, its economic policies pose an equally significant threat to the stability and prosperity of the United States. The foundation's support for unfettered capitalism, tax cuts for the wealthy, and deregulation has contributed to the erosion of the middle class, the hollowing out of public services, and the exacerbation of income inequality. One of the most dangerous aspects of the Heritage Foundation's economic agenda is its push for the privatization of social services. The foundation has advocated for the privatization of Social Security, Medicare, and public education, arguing that market-based solutions are more efficient and effective than government programs. However, the reality is that privatization often leads to higher costs, reduced access, and poorer outcomes for the most vulnerable members of society. By dismantling the social safety net, the Heritage Foundation's policies would leave millions of Americans without the support they need to survive and thrive.

Moreover, the foundation's advocacy for deregulation has had devastating consequences for both the environment and the economy. By rolling back environmental protections and regulatory safeguards, the Heritage Foundation has contributed to the degradation of natural resources, the pollution of air and water, and the acceleration of climate change. These policies not only threaten the health and well-being of current and future generations but also pose significant economic risks, as the costs of environmental damage and climate-related disasters continue to mount. The Heritage Foundation's tax policies are another area of concern. The foundation has consistently pushed for tax cuts for the wealthy and corporations, arguing that this will spur economic growth and create jobs. However, these tax cuts have instead led to massive budget deficits, forcing cuts to essential services and programs that benefit ordinary Americans. The foundation's policies have also contributed to the growing concentration of wealth and power in the hands of a few, undermining the principles of democracy and fairness that are supposed to underpin the American economy.

The Heritage Foundation's history, hypocrisy, and dangerous Christo-fascist agenda represent a significant threat to both the free society and the economic stability of the United States. By promoting policies that curtail civil liberties, undermine democratic principles, and exacerbate economic inequality, the foundation is working to reshape America in its image—one that is authoritarian, exclusionary, and deeply unequal. If left unchecked, the Heritage Foundation's agenda will not only erode the rights and freedoms of women, minorities, and marginalized communities but also wreck the economy by dismantling the social safety net, increasing inequality, and undermining the public institutions that are essential to a healthy and prosperous society. It is imperative that Americans recognize the true nature of the Heritage Foundation's agenda and mobilize to protect the values of democracy, equality, and justice that are fundamental to the nation's identity.

The Heritage Foundation's Project 2025 is not merely a plan for a single election cycle; it represents a long-term agenda aimed at fundamentally reshaping the American government and society into a theocratic state. This blueprint outlines an extensive strategy to systematically dismantle existing democratic institutions and replace them with policies that reflect a rigid, conservative "Christian" ideology. The Foundation's goals go beyond short-term political gains, focusing instead on embedding their values into the very fabric of the nation through sustained efforts. Their agenda includes rolling back civil liberties, restricting reproductive rights, weakening LGBTQ+ protections, and promoting religious freedom laws that prioritize "Christian" beliefs over others. By placing loyalists in key government positions, reducing the size of federal agencies, and privatizing public services, the Heritage Foundation aims to create a government that is smaller in size but vastly more influential in enforcing a conservative, religious agenda.

As extreme "Christian" groups did with the decades long plan to overturn Roe v. Wade, this methodical approach reflects a calculated effort to chip away at the separation of church and state, gradually eroding the pluralistic foundations of American democracy. Project 2025 and the Republican agenda is a strategic vision for the long haul, with the ultimate goal of establishing a government that aligns with their theocratic ideals, undermining the diverse and secular nature of the nation.

Overlapping Key Members of the Heritage Foundation, Project 2025 Architects, and the Trump Administration

1. Kay Coles James, Heritage Foundation: Former President.
   - Director of the U.S. Office of Personnel Management.

2. Chad Wolf, Heritage Foundation: Senior Fellow.
   - Acting Secretary of Homeland Security.

3. Thomas Homan, Heritage Foundation: Visiting Fellow.
   - Acting Director of U.S. Immigration and Customs Enforcement.

4. Mike Pompeo, Heritage Foundation: Frequent consultant.
   - Secretary of State, Director of the CIA.

5. Stephen Moore, Heritage Foundation: Visiting Fellow.
   - Adviser on economic policy, Federal Reserve Board.

6. Robert Bluey, Heritage Foundation: VP of Communications.
   - Influencer and communications strategist.

7. Ken Cuccinelli, Heritage Foundation: Senior Fellow.
   - Acting Director of U.S. Citizenship and Immigration Services.

8. Mark Meadows, Heritage Foundation: Speaker and consultant.
   - White House Chief of Staff.

9. Gene Scalia, Heritage Foundation: Speaker and consultant.
   - Secretary of Labor.

10. Larry Kudlow, Heritage Foundation: Frequent Contributor.
    - Director of the National Economic Council.

These individuals, just ten out of hundreds, represent the significant and compromised overlap between the Heritage Foundation, the architects of Project 2025, and the Trump Administration, highlighting the deep connections and shared ideologies that have influenced "conservative" policymaking in recent years.

Timeline of the New Apostolic Reformation

The New Apostolic Reformation (NAR) is a movement within evangelical Christianity that has grown significantly in influence and reach over the past few decades. Emerging in the late 20th century, the NAR is not a formal denomination but rather a loose network of churches and ministries that share a common theology centered on modern-day apostles and prophets who claim to receive direct revelations from God. These leaders believe they are called to restore what they see as the lost offices of apostle and prophet, and to lead the church, through a Project 2025 agenda in dominion over all aspects of society, including government, education, and the economy.

The origins of the NAR can be traced to figures like C. Peter Wagner, a money hungry power obsessed radical and former professor at Fuller Theological Seminary, who coined the term "New Apostolic Reformation" in the late 1990s. Wagner and his contemporaries argued that the traditional structures of the church were insufficient to bring about the global spiritual revival they believed was necessary for the return of Jesus Christ. Instead, they advocated for a new model of church leadership, one that emphasized the authority of fake apostles and fake prophets to guide and direct the church in spiritual warfare against what they viewed as the forces of evil in society.

This movement quickly gained traction among charismatic and Pentecostal Christians, particularly in the United States. The NAR's emphasis on spiritual warfare, prophecy, and miraculous healing resonated with believers who were disillusioned with traditional church structures and were seeking a more direct and experiential connection with the divine. Over time, the NAR's influence expanded beyond the church, as its leaders began to see themselves as agents of cultural and political change, tasked with transforming society to reflect their interpretation of "Christian" values.

Project 2025, is deeply intertwined with the ideology and goals of the New Apostolic Reformation. The NAR's leaders and adherents have increasingly positioned themselves as key players in the broader conservative movement, particularly in the United States. They see the political sphere as a crucial battleground in their spiritual warfare and have sought to align themselves with like-minded politicians and organizations to advance their agenda.

The connection between the NAR and Project 2025 can be seen in several ways. First, many of the policy goals outlined in Project 2025 align closely with the NAR's vision of a Christian-dominated society. The NAR's influence is also evident in the emphasis on religious education and school choice, which reflect the movement's desire to shape the next generation with its values. Furthermore, the NAR's strategy of engaging in political and cultural battles to achieve their vision of a "Christian" society mirrors the objectives of Project 2025. The movement's leaders often speak of the "Seven Mountain Mandate," a belief that "Christians" are called to dominate seven key areas of society: government, education, media, arts and entertainment, family, religion, and business. This mandate is reflected in the broad scope of Project 2025, which seeks to reshape American society across multiple domains.

The involvement of NAR leaders in conservative political circles and their connections to influential think tanks and advocacy groups suggest that their influence on Project 2025 is not merely theoretical but practical. These leaders have increasingly found themselves in advisory roles or as allies to political figures who share their vision, thus embedding their ideology within the broader conservative movement.

The rise of the New Apostolic Reformation and its influence on political projects like Project 2025 is concerning for several reasons, particularly regarding the movement's approach to governance, civil liberties, and religious pluralism. Firstly, the NAR's belief in modern-day apostles and prophets who claim direct revelations from God presents a significant challenge to democratic principles and the rule of law. In a secular democracy, laws and policies are ideally based on reason, debate, and the will of the people. However, the NAR's leaders believe they are divinely appointed to enact God's will on earth, which can lead to a form of governance that is authoritarian and resistant to accountability. When political leaders are influenced by or beholden to figures who claim divine authority, there is a risk that decisions will be made based on dogma rather than democratic deliberation.

Secondly, the NAR's vision of societal transformation through the

"Seven Mountain Mandate" is inherently exclusionary and threatens religious freedom and pluralism. By seeking to dominate key areas of society, the NAR's agenda does not allow for the coexistence of diverse beliefs and values. This approach is likely to lead to policies that privilege one particular religious perspective at the expense of others, undermining the constitutional separation of church and state and marginalizing those who do not conform to the NAR's vision of Christianity. The movement's leaders have been vocal in their opposition to same-sex marriage, transgender rights, and abortion, often framing these issues as part of a larger spiritual battle. Their influence on projects like Project 2025 suggests that these views could translate into policies that roll back hard-won rights and freedoms for vulnerable communities.

The NAR's focus on spiritual warfare and its apocalyptic worldview also contribute to its potential for danger. By framing political and cultural conflicts as battles between good and evil, the NAR encourages a zero-sum approach to governance that leaves little room for compromise or dialogue. This mentality can lead to increased polarization and conflict within society, as well as the justification of extreme measures to achieve the movement's goals. Lastly, the NAR's influence on education is particularly concerning. The movement's leaders advocate for religious education and the inclusion of "Christian" teachings in public schools, which threatens the secular nature of the American education system, undermining the quality of public education, and indoctrinating future generations with its ideology.

The New Apostolic Reformation represents a significant and growing force within the American conservative movement, one that is increasingly shaping political agendas like Project 2025. The movement's emphasis on divine authority, its exclusionary vision for society, and its aggressive stance on social issues make it a particularly dangerous entity. If the NAR's influence continues to grow, the result could be a society that is less free, less inclusive, and less democratic— a society where governance is based not on the rule of law and democratic principles, but on the dogmatic beliefs of a select few. The rise of the New Apostolic Reformation is a reminder of the importance of vigilance in protecting the values of religious pluralism, civil liberties, and democratic governance.

Timeline of Christian Wars

Christianity, founded over two millennia ago, began as a religion rooted in the teachings of love, compassion, and peace as exemplified by Jesus Christ. However, over the centuries, this faith has undergone significant transformations, often diverging from its original teachings. Today, Christianity in some circles has become entangled in culture wars, where its message is often used as a weapon in political and social battles. This timeline traces the historical evolution of Christianity, highlighting key moments that led to the current state where the faith is often associated with division, conflict, and control as seen in Project 2025, rather than its original message of peace.

1st Century AD: The Birth of Christianity

Christianity emerged in the 1st century AD, rooted in the teachings of Jesus of Nazareth, who preached love, forgiveness, and compassion. His message was revolutionary for its time, focusing on the marginalized and emphasizing a personal relationship with God over strict adherence to religious laws. After Jesus' crucifixion and resurrection, his followers spread his teachings, forming the early Christian Church. These early Christians were often persecuted for their beliefs but remained steadfast in their commitment to peace and non-violence, even in the face of oppression.

4th Century AD: The Conversion of Constantine and the Roman Empire

The 4th century marked a significant turning point for Christianity when Emperor Constantine converted to the faith and declared it the official religion of the Roman Empire. This event, known as the Edict of Milan in 313 AD, ended the persecution of Christians and began the process of Christianity becoming intertwined with political power. While this shift allowed the faith to spread more rapidly, it also marked the beginning of its transformation from a grassroots movement of peace to an institution of power. The fusion of church and state introduced new challenges, as the Christian message was sometimes co-opted to justify political agendas, including military conquests.

Middle Ages: The Crusades and the Rise of Christendom

During the Middle Ages, Christianity's association with power became more pronounced, particularly during the Crusades (1096-1291 AD). These religious wars, sanctioned by the Church, aimed to reclaim the Holy Land from Muslim control and were marked by extreme violence and the spread of Christianity through force. The Crusades represented a stark departure from the peaceful teachings of Jesus and highlighted the growing corruption within the Church, where spiritual goals were often overshadowed by political and territorial ambitions.

Simultaneously, the concept of Christendom—a political and religious unity of Christian states—emerged. The Church became a dominant force in European life, dictating not only religious practices but also political and social norms. This period saw the consolidation of the Church's power but also a growing disconnect between the teachings of Christ and the actions of the Christian institutions.

16th Century: The Protestant Reformation

The Protestant Reformation in the 16th century was a response to the perceived corruption and moral decay within the Catholic Church. Figures like Martin Luther and John Calvin challenged the authority of the Pope and criticized practices such as the sale of indulgences. The Reformation led to the splintering of Christianity into multiple denominations, each interpreting the teachings of Jesus differently.

While the Reformation aimed to return Christianity to its more authentic roots, it also led to religious wars and conflicts, such as the Thirty Years' War (1618-1648). These conflicts further entrenched the use of Christianity as a tool for political power, rather than a message of peace and reconciliation.

18th-19th Century: The Enlightenment and the *Separation of Church and State

The Enlightenment of the 18th century introduced new ideas about reason, science, and the separation of church and state. In the United States, the First Amendment enshrined the principle of religious freedom, preventing the establishment of a national religion and protecting individuals' rights to practice their faith freely.

During this period, many Christian movements in the United States, such as the abolitionist movement, used the faith's teachings to advocate for social justice and human rights. However, the relationship between Christianity and political power persisted, particularly in the South, where the Bible was often used to justify slavery.

20th Century: The Rise of the Religious Right

The 20th century saw the rise of the Religious Right, particularly in the United States, where conservative Christian groups began to exert significant influence on politics. This movement gained momentum in the 1970s, with figures like Jerry Falwell and organizations such as the Moral Majority mobilizing Christians to support conservative causes and candidates.

The Religious Right framed many political issues, such as abortion, gay rights, and school prayer, as moral battles, often positioning themselves as defenders of Christian values against a perceived secular onslaught. This period marked the beginning of the modern culture wars, where Christianity became increasingly associated with conservative politics and social conservatism.

21st Century: Christianity and Today's Culture Wars

In the 21st century, Christianity's role in the culture wars has only intensified. Issues like LGBTQ+ rights, abortion, immigration, and religious freedom are often at the center of these conflicts, with Christian rhetoric frequently used to justify positions on both sides. However, the use of Christianity in these debates has sometimes led to a distortion of the faith's core teachings.

For example, the use of Christian teachings to oppose same-sex marriage and LGBTQ+ rights often overlooks the message of love and acceptance that is central to Jesus' teachings. Similarly, the opposition to abortion rights, while rooted in a sincere belief in the sanctity of life, has sometimes led to violent actions and rhetoric that are far removed from the peaceful teachings of Christ.

Moreover, the alignment of Christianity with nationalist and exclusionary ideologies, particularly in movements like Christian nationalism, has further corrupted the faith's message. These movements often promote a vision of America as a Christian nation, where religious and cultural homogeneity is prioritized over pluralism and diversity. This approach not only undermines the separation of church and state but also alienates those who do not share these views, leading to increased polarization and conflict.

Present Day Corruption of Christianity's Message

The current state of Christianity, particularly within the context of the culture wars, represents a significant departure from its origins. The faith that once preached peace, love, and compassion has been co-opted in many instances to serve political ends, often leading to division and conflict rather than reconciliation and understanding.

This corruption is not only detrimental to the broader society but also to the integrity of Christianity itself. When the faith is used as a weapon in political battles, its message is diluted, and its credibility is undermined. This shift has also led to a growing number of people, particularly younger generations, distancing themselves from organized religion, seeing it as more concerned with politics than with spiritual growth or social justice. As Christianity continues to be entangled in the culture wars, there is a growing need for reflection within the faith community. The core teachings of Jesus—love your neighbor, care for the poor and marginalized, and seek peace—should serve as a guiding light in these tumultuous times. The history of Christianity shows that it has often strayed from these principles, but it also shows that the faith has the capacity for renewal and transformation.

To move forward, Christians must reclaim their faith from those who would use it to divide rather than unite, to harm rather than heal. By returning to the teachings of Christ, Christianity can once again become a force for peace and justice in the world, rather than a source of conflict and division. In doing so, it can help to heal the wounds of the culture wars and build a more inclusive, compassionate society.

Separation of Church and State

The principle of separating church and state is a cornerstone of modern democracy, rooted deeply in the vision of America's Founding Fathers. This separation ensures that government remains neutral in religious matters, thereby protecting individual freedoms and maintaining a society where diverse beliefs can coexist peacefully.

Thomas Jefferson, one of the foremost advocates for this principle, famously wrote in his 1802 letter to the Danbury Baptist Association, "I contemplate with sovereign reverence that act of the whole American people which declared that their legislature should 'make no law respecting an establishment of religion, or prohibiting the free exercise thereof,' thus building a wall of separation between Church and State." Jefferson's words reflect the deep commitment to preventing any single religion from dominating government policy, which he believed was essential for safeguarding liberty.

James Madison, often called the "Father of the Constitution," also emphasized the importance of this separation. He warned against the dangers of intertwining government and religion, stating, "The purpose of separation of church and state is to keep forever from these shores the ceaseless strife that has soaked the soil of Europe in blood for centuries." Madison's perspective was shaped by his understanding of European history, where religious conflicts had led to prolonged wars and persecution.

George Washington, in his famous letter to the Hebrew Congregation of Newport in 1790, affirmed the nation's commitment to religious liberty, saying, "The government of the United States... gives to bigotry no sanction, to persecution no assistance." Washington's words underline the belief that the government should not favor one religion over another, that faiths thrive without fear of oppression.

These quotes from the Founding Fathers illustrate that the separation of church and state is not merely a legal doctrine but a fundamental principle that ensures the protection of individual rights and the promotion of a pluralistic society. This separation upholds the freedom of conscience and prevents the government from becoming an instrument of religious coercion, thus preserving the integrity of both religion and government in a diverse democracy.

Project 2025 Contributors

Alabama Policy Institute
Alliance Defending Freedom
America First Legal
American Accountability Foundation
American Association of Pro-Life Obstetricians and Gynecologists
ACLJ Action
American Compass
American Cornerstone Institute
American Council of Trustees and Alumni
American Family Association
American Family Project
American Legislative Exchange Council
American Juris Link
AMAC Action
American Moment
American Principles Project
California Family Council
Center for Equal Opportunity
Center for Family and Human Rights
Center for Immigration Studies
Center for Renewing America
Claremont Institute
Coalition for a Prosperous America
Competitive Enterprise Institute
Concerned Women for America
Conservative Partnership Institute
Defense of Freedom Institute
Ethics and Public Policy Center
Family Policy Alliance
Family Research Council
Feds for Medical Freedom
First Liberty Institute
Forge Leadership Network
Foundation for American Innovation
Foundation for Defense of Democracies
Foundation for Government Accountability
Frederick Douglass Foundation
FreedomWorks
Heartland Institute
Heritage Foundation
Hillsdale College
Honest Elections Project
Independent Women's Forum

Institute for Education Reform
Institute for Energy Research
Institute for the American Worker
Institute for Women's Health
Intercollegiate Studies Institute
James Madison Institute
Job Creators Network
Keystone Policy
Liberty University
Media Research Center
Mississippi Center for Public Policy
Moms for Liberty
National Association of Scholars
National Center for Public Policy Research
Noah Webster Educational Foundation
Oklahoma Council of Public Affairs
Pacific Research Institute
Patrick Henry College
Personnel Policy Operations
Project 21 Black Leadership Network
Public Interest Legal Foundation
Recovery for America Now Foundation
Susan B. Anthony Pro-Life America
Tea Party Patriots
Teneo Network
Texas Public Policy Foundation
The American Conservative
The American Main Street Initiative
The Leadership Institute
Turning Point USA
Young America's Foundation
1792 Exchange

These organizations, with their far right patriarchal, racist, and religious views, use economic agendas to overshadow their regressive goals of overturning a century of progress for women and minorities. By aggressively pushing for deregulation, tax cuts for the wealthy, and reduced government oversight, they mask their underlying intention to dismantle protections and rights that have been hard-won over decades. Their economic policies promise growth and prosperity, but in reality, they often lead to increased inequality, disproportionately affecting women and minorities who rely on social services and regulatory protections to ensure fair treatment and opportunities in the workplace and society. These are organizations to distrust.

Individual Millionaire and Billionaire Backers

Estimates suggest that well over $100 million dollars has been funneled into Project 2025. It is backed by some of the wealthiest individuals and families in the United States, many of whom are known for their extensive influence in conservative politics. These are traitors to America and what she stands for. Here are 25 of the top millionaire and billionaire backers, listed in order of contribution:

Leonard Leo - Known for his extensive work in reshaping the judiciary, Leo has funneled millions through dark money networks in support.

Charles Koch - The Koch network has directed over $4.4 million to Project 2025, emphasizing deregulation and conservative energy policies.

Harlan Crow - A Texas real estate magnate, Crow has been a significant donor to conservative causes and Project 2025.

Paul Singer - A hedge fund billionaire, Singer has heavily financed conservative initiatives, including those under Project 2025.

Robert Mercer - The hedge fund manager and prominent Trump supporter has contributed substantially to the project.

Rebekah Mercer - Robert Mercer's daughter, also a major conservative donor, heavily involved in funding Project 2025.

Ken Griffin - The billionaire hedge fund manager has been a notable contributor to various conservative causes.

Sheldon Adelson - Before his death, Adelson was a major GOP donor, with his estate continuing to support conservative agendas.

Richard Uihlein - The Uline CEO has been a prolific donor to right-wing causes and candidates.

Betsy DeVos - The former Education Secretary and her family are long-time supporters of conservative education reform and Project 2025.

Peter Thiel - The tech billionaire and Trump supporter has funded numerous conservative projects, including Project 2025.

Joe Ricketts - Founder of TD Ameritrade, Ricketts has been a significant funder of conservative initiatives.

Timothy Mellon - Heir to the Mellon fortune, he has donated millions to conservative causes.

Bernard Marcus - Co-founder of Home Depot, Marcus has been a major financial backer of conservative policies.

Foster Friess - The late investor and philanthropist was known for his generous donations to conservative causes.

Phil Anschutz - A billionaire with deep investments in conservative media and political movements.

Isaac Perlmutter - Former Marvel CEO, Perlmutter has been a significant donor to conservative campaigns.

Bruce Kovner - A hedge fund billionaire who has supported numerous conservative think tanks and initiatives.

Dick DeVos - Betsy DeVos' husband, also a significant funder of conservative education reform.

Thomas Wachtell - An investor known for his substantial contributions to conservative political causes.

Ron Cameron - Agribusiness tycoon, Cameron has been a major donor to right-wing political movements.

Sanford Diller - The late real estate mogul was a prominent supporter of conservative causes.

George Roberts - Co-founder of global investment company KKR, Roberts has contributed extensively to conservative political campaigns.

Jeffrey Yass - A financier who has donated millions to conservative political action committees.

Randy Kendrick - The wife of Arizona Diamondbacks owner Ken Kendrick, she has been a major donor to conservative causes.

Note on Greed

In contemporary American politics and society, there is a troubling alignment between certain "Christian" organizations and Republican public servants. This coalition, often cloaked in the language of morality, faith, and public service, has increasingly demonstrated behavior driven by greed and self-interest. This greed not only stands in stark contrast to the foundational principles of Christianity, such as compassion, humility, and service to others, but also has destructive consequences for the social fabric and economic well-being of the nation. Many "Christian" organizations, particularly those aligned with right-wing politics, have become vehicles for accumulating wealth rather than serving their communities. These organizations often exploit religious rhetoric to solicit donations, amass wealth, and exert influence over public policy. This behavior is perhaps most visible in the practices of prominent televangelists who preach the "prosperity gospel," a doctrine that suggests financial success is a sign of divine favor and that donating to their ministries will result in material blessings for the giver.

Televangelists like Joel Osteen, Kenneth Copeland, and Paula White have built multi-million-dollar empires by appealing to the religious devotion of their followers. They promise their audiences that financial contributions to their ministries will result in divine rewards, often suggesting that faith and generosity will lead to personal wealth. However, the wealth accumulated by these religious leaders is frequently spent on lavish lifestyles, including mansions, private jets, and luxury cars, which starkly contrast with the teachings of Jesus, who emphasized humility, charity, and care for the poor. This exploitation of faith not only betrays the trust of their followers but also distorts the message of Christianity. The prosperity gospel, which equates material wealth with spiritual favor, undermines the Christian principles of selflessness and service to others. By focusing on personal gain and wealth accumulation, these organizations contribute to a culture of materialism and self-interest that is antithetical to the core tenets of Christianity.

Moreover, the greed of these organizations has broader societal implications. By diverting funds that could be used for charitable work or community support, these organizations fail to address the real needs of the communities they claim to serve. Instead of investing in programs that alleviate poverty, provide education, or offer healthcare, these funds are often used to maintain the extravagant lifestyles of their leaders. This behavior not only harms the individuals who are manipulated into giving but also deprives society of the benefits that could come from more ethically managed religious organizations. The greed that characterizes many "Christian" organizations is mirrored in the actions of Republican public servants, who often prioritize the interests of the wealthy and powerful over the needs of their constituents. Under the guise of promoting economic freedom and limited government, these politicians have consistently supported policies that disproportionately benefit the rich, exacerbating income inequality and social division.

One of the most glaring examples is the Republican Party's commitment to tax cuts for the wealthy. Since the Reagan era, the party has championed "trickle-down economics," the idea that cutting taxes for the rich will stimulate economic growth and ultimately benefit everyone. However, decades of evidence have shown that these policies primarily serve to enrich the already wealthy, with little benefit to the broader population. The 2017 Tax Cuts and Jobs Act, for example, provided substantial tax breaks to corporations and high-income individuals while offering minimal relief to middle- and lower-income Americans. This policy has contributed to widening the wealth gap, undermining public services, and creating long-term fiscal challenges that will burden future generations.

In addition to tax policies, Republican lawmakers have consistently sought to deregulate industries, particularly in the financial and environmental sectors. These deregulatory efforts are often framed as promoting business freedom and economic growth, but they primarily serve the interests of large corporations and wealthy donors. The rollback of financial regulations, for instance, played a significant role in the 2008 financial crisis, which caused widespread economic harm to ordinary Americans while largely sparing the wealthy and powerful. Similarly, efforts to dismantle environmental protections have benefited fossil fuel companies and other polluting industries at the expense of public health and environmental sustainability. By prioritizing corporate profits over the well-being of the planet and its inhabitants, Republican lawmakers are perpetuating a cycle of greed that has long-term destructive consequences for both people and the planet.

The greed of "Christian" organizations and Republican public servants is also evident in their approach to social services and public welfare. Many of these entities advocate for the reduction or elimination of government programs that provide essential services to vulnerable populations, arguing that such programs create dependency and stifle personal responsibility. However, this rhetoric often serves as a cover for policies that prioritize tax cuts for the wealthy over investments in public goods.

For example, Republican lawmakers have repeatedly attempted to cut funding for programs like Medicaid, food stamps, and affordable housing. These cuts are often justified on the grounds of reducing government spending, but in reality, they reflect a lack of concern for the well-being of those who rely on these services. By depriving people of the support they need to survive and thrive, these policies exacerbate poverty and inequality while further enriching those who are already financially secure. The same pattern is evident in the approach to healthcare. The Republican Party has consistently sought to repeal or undermine the Affordable Care Act (ACA), which expanded access to healthcare for millions of Americans. Despite claiming to support healthcare reform, many Republican lawmakers have failed to propose viable alternatives that would ensure continued coverage for those who gained insurance through the ACA. Instead, their proposals have often focused on reducing government involvement in healthcare, which would likely lead to higher costs and reduced access for millions of Americans.

This approach to social services and public welfare reflects a broader ideological commitment to shrinking the role of government, even when doing so harms vulnerable populations. By prioritizing tax cuts and deregulation over investments in public goods, Republican public servants are advancing a vision of society where the wealthy are protected, and the poor are left to fend for themselves. This vision is not only morally problematic but also economically shortsighted, as it undermines the social stability and economic mobility that are essential for a healthy and prosperous society. The greed that drives these "Christian" organizations and Republican public servants has far-reaching consequences, both morally and socially. It erodes trust in public institutions, fosters cynicism and disengagement from the political process, and undermines the values of community and solidarity that are essential for a healthy society. When leaders prioritize wealth and power over the common good, they create a society marked by inequality, division, and injustice.

One of the most troubling aspects of this greed is the way it distorts the values that should guide both religious and public life. Christianity, at its core, teaches principles of love, compassion, and service to others. Yet, when "Christian" organizations and their leaders prioritize wealth accumulation and material success, they betray these values and contribute to a culture of greed and self-interest. This culture not only dehumanizes individuals but also undermines the sense of shared responsibility that is necessary for addressing the many challenges facing society, from poverty and inequality to climate change and public health.

Moreover, the emphasis on wealth as a measure of success and virtue distorts the political landscape as well. When Republican public servants prioritize the interests of the wealthy and powerful over the needs of their constituents, they undermine the principles of democracy and equality that are supposed to underpin American society. By catering to the interests of a small elite, they contribute to the erosion of trust in public institutions and the polarization of the political system. This erosion of trust is particularly damaging in a democracy, where the legitimacy of the government depends on the consent and confidence of the governed. When people perceive that their leaders are more interested in serving the interests of the wealthy than in addressing the needs of the broader population, they become disillusioned and disengaged from the political process. This disengagement weakens the democratic system and makes it more difficult to address the pressing challenges facing society.

The media also plays a significant role in perpetuating the greed of these organizations and public servants. Many conservative media outlets, aligned with these interests, have helped shape public discourse in ways that obscure the true nature of the greed and self-interest driving many policies. These outlets often promote narratives that glorify wealth accumulation and demonize government intervention, framing social programs as wasteful and inefficient while downplaying the benefits they provide to society. This manipulation of public discourse has far-reaching consequences. By shaping public perceptions and attitudes, the media can influence the political landscape and the policies that are enacted. When the public is fed a steady diet of misinformation and distorted narratives, it becomes more difficult to build the broad-based support needed to address issues like income inequality, healthcare, and environmental protection. Instead, these issues are framed as divisive and polarizing, making it more difficult to find common ground and enact meaningful change.

At the heart of the problem is a failure of moral leadership. Both religious leaders and public servants have a responsibility to act in the best interests of their communities and to uphold the values of justice, compassion, and service. When they instead prioritize their own wealth and power, they betray this responsibility and contribute to a culture of greed and self-interest that is corrosive to the social fabric. This failure of leadership is particularly troubling in the context of Christianity, which teaches that those in positions of power have a duty to serve others and to care for the vulnerable. When religious leaders exploit their followers for financial gain, they not only betray their congregations but also undermine the credibility of the faith they claim to represent. This behavior is not only morally wrong but also deeply damaging to the spiritual health of their communities.

Similarly, when public servants prioritize the interests of the wealthy and powerful over the needs of their constituents, they betray the principles of democracy and equality that are supposed to guide their actions. This betrayal has far-reaching consequences, as it undermines trust in public institutions and fuels a growing sense of disillusionment and alienation among the populace. As trust in government and religious institutions erodes, so too does the foundation of social cohesion and shared responsibility that is essential for a functioning democracy. This sense of betrayal can lead to apathy and cynicism, weakening the bonds that hold communities together and making it more difficult to mobilize collective action for the common good.

The economic implications of the greed exhibited by these "Christian" organizations and Republican public servants are also profound. Policies that prioritize tax cuts for the wealthy and deregulation at the expense of social services and public welfare contribute to growing income inequality and economic instability. This approach to governance is not only morally questionable but also economically unsustainable. By funneling wealth to the top echelons of society while stripping away the social safety nets that protect the most vulnerable, these policies create a deeply imbalanced economy. The concentration of wealth in the hands of a few reduces consumer spending, which is a key driver of economic growth. When ordinary people struggle to afford basic necessities like healthcare, housing, and education, their ability to participate fully in the economy is diminished, leading to slower economic growth and reduced opportunities for upward mobility.

Moreover, the emphasis on deregulation often leads to short-term gains for corporations and investors at the expense of long-term economic health. For example, deregulating environmental protections may boost profits for polluting industries in the short term, but it also leads to environmental degradation that imposes significant costs on society in the long run. The resulting damage to public health, infrastructure, and natural resources ultimately harms the economy and reduces the quality of life for all. The weakening of public institutions and services also undermines economic stability. When healthcare, education, and social services are underfunded or privatized, the quality and accessibility of these essential services decline, creating barriers to economic opportunity and exacerbating social inequality. This dynamic creates a vicious cycle, where the wealthy and powerful continue to accumulate more resources and influence, while the rest of society is left to bear the burden of an increasingly unequal and unjust system.

Addressing the greed that pervades these "Christian" organizations and Republican public servants requires a fundamental shift in values and priorities. It necessitates a reawakening of the ethical imperatives that should guide both religious and political leadership—namely, a commitment to justice, compassion, and the common good. For religious organizations, this means returning to the core teachings of Christianity, which emphasize love, humility, and service to others. Religious leaders must reject the prosperity gospel and other doctrines that equate wealth with spiritual favor, and instead focus on addressing the needs of the poor, the marginalized, and the oppressed. By doing so, they can restore the integrity of their faith and contribute to the healing of the social fabric.

For public servants, this means placing the well-being of their constituents above the interests of wealthy donors and corporate lobbyists. Policymakers must prioritize investments in social services, healthcare, education, and infrastructure, recognizing that these are not just expenses but essential foundations for a thriving society. They must also commit to creating a fairer tax system that ensures the wealthy pay their fair share, and to enacting regulations that protect the environment, public health, and economic stability.

The path forward requires a collective effort to build a more just and equitable society, one that is grounded in the principles of fairness, responsibility, and mutual respect. This effort must involve not only holding leaders accountable for their actions but also fostering a broader cultural shift away from greed and materialism. One important step is to support and amplify voices within both the religious and political spheres that advocate for these values. There are many faith leaders and public servants who are committed to justice and compassion, and their work must be recognized and supported. At the same time, it is crucial to challenge and resist those who prioritize wealth and power over the common good.

Education and public awareness are also key components of this effort. By raising awareness of the destructive impact of greed-driven policies and the ethical failings of certain leaders, we can empower individuals and communities to demand change. This includes advocating for policies that promote economic justice, environmental sustainability, and social equity, as well as supporting organizations and initiatives that work to address these issues. The greed that drives many "Christian" organizations and Republican public servants is not just a moral failing; it is a systemic problem with deep implications for society. It erodes trust in institutions, exacerbates inequality, and undermines the values that are essential for a healthy and just society. Addressing this greed requires holding leaders accountable, to promote ethical leadership, and to build a culture that values compassion, justice, and the common good over wealth and power.

Ultimately, the challenge is not just to confront the greed of certain individuals or organizations, but to transform the systems and structures that enable and perpetuate this greed. By doing so, we can create a society where everyone has the opportunity to thrive, where public servants truly serve the public, and where religious organizations live up to the values they profess. This is not just an ethical imperative but a practical necessity for building a more equitable, sustainable, and prosperous future for all.

In Conclusion

As we stand on the precipice of an uncertain future, it is imperative to examine the chilling implications of Project 2025. This ambitious endeavor, championed by Republicans, the Heritage Foundation, and its allies, aims to reshape the American political landscape in ways that could have devastating consequences for our democracy, our economy, and our very way of life. Project 2025 is not merely a collection of policy proposals; it is a blueprint for a Christo-fascist ideology that seeks to impose a theocratic vision on our secular republic, while simultaneously advancing the interests of unbridled capitalism and promoting a relentless agenda of deregulation.

At its core, Project 2025 is driven by a Christo-fascist ideology that seeks to merge religious dogma with state power. This vision is deeply rooted in the belief that America is a Christian nation and that its laws and policies should reflect a specific interpretation of "Christian" values. This perspective is profoundly anti-democratic, as it seeks to impose a singular religious viewpoint on a pluralistic society. It threatens the separation of church and state, a foundational principle of our democracy, and undermines the religious freedom of all Americans, particularly those who adhere to different faiths or none at all. The proponents of Project 2025 argue that their vision is about restoring moral order and defending traditional values. However, this rhetoric masks a more insidious agenda. The Christo-fascist ideology embedded in Project 2025 seeks to roll back hard-won rights and freedoms, particularly for women, LGBTQ+ individuals, and religious minorities. It envisions a society where religious conformity is enforced through the power of the state, where dissent is suppressed, and theocratic leaders dictate the terms of public and private life.

This ideology is not only about imposing a particular set of religious beliefs but also about consolidating power in the hands of a select few. It is deeply intertwined with a broader agenda of capitalism and deregulation, which seeks to dismantle the regulatory state and unleash the full force of market fundamentalism. The economic vision of Project 2025 is one of unfettered capitalism, where the interests of corporations and the wealthy are prioritized over the needs of ordinary Americans.

The deregulatory agenda of Project 2025 and the Republicans aims to roll back critical protections for workers, consumers, and the environment. This vision is rooted in the belief that government intervention is inherently harmful and that the free market should be the primary arbiter of economic and social outcomes. However, this perspective ignores the profound inequalities and injustices that arise in an unregulated market. It fails to acknowledge the essential role that government plays in safeguarding public health, protecting the environment, and ensuring fair labor practices. Under the guise of promoting economic freedom, Project 2025 seeks to dismantle the regulatory frameworks that have been established to protect the public from corporate abuses. It envisions a world where environmental regulations are gutted, allowing polluters to ravage our natural resources and poison our communities without consequence. It aims to weaken labor protections, making it easier for employers to exploit workers and undermine their rights to fair wages, safe working conditions, and collective bargaining. It seeks to roll back consumer protections, leaving individuals vulnerable to predatory practices and corporate malfeasance.

The economic policies of Project 2025 and the Republicans are not about creating a level playing field or promoting genuine prosperity for all. Instead, they are designed to entrench the power and wealth of a privileged few at the expense of the many. This vision of capitalism is one that is devoid of compassion, equity, and justice. It prioritizes profit over people and seeks to create a society where the wealthy and powerful can operate with impunity, free from the constraints of regulation and accountability. The confluence of Christo-fascist ideology and unbridled capitalism in Project 2025 represents a profound threat to the principles of democracy, justice, and equality. This project seeks to reshape our institutions and policies in ways that will erode the rights and freedoms of ordinary Americans and entrench the power of a privileged elite. It is a vision that is profoundly anti-democratic, as it seeks to concentrate power in the hands of a few and impose a singular religious and economic orthodoxy on a diverse and pluralistic society.

In conclusion, Project 2025 is a dangerous and far-reaching agenda that threatens to undermine the very foundations of our democracy. It seeks to impose a Christo-fascist ideology that is at odds with the principles of religious freedom and pluralism. It promotes an economic vision of unfettered capitalism that prioritizes the interests of the wealthy and powerful over the needs of ordinary Americans. And it advances a deregulatory agenda that threatens to roll back critical protections for workers, consumers, and the environment. As we look to the future, it is essential that we remain vigilant in defending the principles of democracy, justice, and equality. We must resist the efforts of those who seek to impose a theocratic vision on our secular republic and who seek to dismantle the regulatory frameworks that protect our rights and well-being. The stakes are too high to remain silent or complacent. We must stand up for the values that define us as a nation and work together to build a future that is inclusive, equitable, and just for all.

By framing their agenda as a quest for economic efficiency and freedom, they divert attention from the social ramifications of their policies. For instance, while advocating for lower taxes and reduced welfare programs, they simultaneously support restrictions on reproductive rights and rollbacks of affirmative action, directly attacking the autonomy and advancement of women and minorities. This strategy of using economic arguments as a smokescreen allows them to pursue a conservative social agenda that threatens to erode the significant gains made in gender and racial equality over the past century. The road ahead will not be easy, and the forces arrayed against us are formidable. But we have faced challenges before, and we have always risen to meet them. By standing together and speaking out against the dangers of Project 2025 and the Republican plan, we can ensure that our democracy remains strong, our rights are protected, and our future is one of hope and opportunity for all. Let us remain steadfast in our commitment to these principles and work tirelessly to create a better, more just world for generations to come.

List of Prints

1.	Note on Section F	12
2.	Note on the Incurious	14
3.	Agriculture	16
4.	Children	20
5.	Climate	24
6.	Crime	28
7.	Education	32
8.	Elections	36
9.	Energy	40
10.	Entertainment	44
11.	Family	48
12.	Finance	52
13.	Government	56
14.	Health	60
15.	Housing	64
16.	Immigration	68
17.	International	72
18.	Justice	76
19.	Labor	80
20.	LGBTQ+	84
21.	Media	88
22.	Men	92
23.	Military	96
24.	Minorities	100
25.	Religion	104
26.	Taxes	108
27.	Technology	112
28.	Transportation	116
29.	Veterans	120
30.	Women	124
31.	Note on Original Sin	128
32.	Note on the Two Santa Clause Theory	132
33.	Note on the GI Bill	136
34.	Timeline of Money in Politics	140
35.	Timeline of The Heritage Foundation	146
36.	Timeline of The New Apostolic Reformation	152
37.	Timeline of Christian Wars	156
38.	Note on Greed	166
39.	In Conclusion	174

About the author

The author lives removed.

Please feel free to burn part or all of this book, safely, as an effigy.

Made in the USA
Columbia, SC
14 September 2024